CATULLUS
VOCABULARY CARDS
for AP Selections*

David R. Pellegrino

Bolchazy-Carducci Publishers, Inc.
Wauconda, Illinois USA

Editor
Laurie Haight Keenan

Cover Design
Adam Phillip Velez

Cover & Title Page Illustration
Orpheus and Eurydice
by Thom Kapheim

Catullus Vocabulary Cards for AP* Selections

David R. Pellegrino

"Meters of the Poems" and "Metrical Terms, Tropes or Figures of Thought, and Rhetorical Figures or Figures of Speech" are by Ronnie Ancona, from *Writing Passion: A Catullus Reader,* © copyright 2004, Bolchazy-Carducci Publishers, Inc.

Graphic Latin Grammar was prepared by James P. Humphreys, © copyright 2005, Bolchazy-Carducci Publishers, Inc., and is available in laminated cardstock from Bolchazy-Carducci Publishers, Inc.

Bolchazy-Carducci Publishers, Inc.
1000 Brown Street
Wauconda, IL 60084 USA
www.bolchazy.com

Printed in the United States of America
2006
by United Graphics

ISBN-13: 978-0-86516-653-0
ISBN-10: 0-86516-653-6

ACKNOWLEDGEMENTS

This book is dedicated to following influential people:

Mrs. Evelyn Dunn, my first Latin teacher,
who instilled in me the love of Latin and teaching

Patricia Gregory, my cooperating teacher at Linton High School
(now Schenectady High School), who inspired me to expect
the best from my students

Pittsford Mendon High School AP Latin students,
who used these materials in their raw form and provided
wonderful feedback

My mother and father, Earlene and Peter Pellegrino,
without whom I would not be where I am today

David R. Pellegrino

15+

ā, ab

15+

ac, átque

15+

ad

15+

ámō, -ā́re, -ā́vī, -ā́tus

15+

ámor, amṓris, *m.*

15+

at

15+

aut
aut...aut

15+

Catúllus, Catúllī, *m.*

15+

cum (*conj.*)

15+

dī́cō, -ere, dī́xī, díctus

and; as

(with *abl.*) from; by

(*ab*-prefix: abduction)

to love

(amatory)

(with *acc.*) to; at; for

(*ad*-prefix: addition)

but

love; lover; Cupid (god of love)

(amorous)

(Gaius Valerius Catullus, lyric poet)

or
either...or

to say, tell; to call

(diction)

when; since; although;
(taken with *prīmum*) as soon as;
(with *tum*) not only

I, me

(egotistic)

out of, from

(*ex*-prefix: exonerate)

to do; to make; to write; to see to it;
to value; to regard; to find

(factor)

and, even
both...and

now, already; (with a negative) longer

this; he, she, it

(with *acc.*) into; upon, to; against; among;
(with *abl.*) in, on, among; at; for

(*in-*, *im-*prefixes: insert, import)

that; he, she, it

bad, evil

(malevolent)

-self; (*f.*) mistress

15+

mēns, méntis, *f.*

15+

méus, -a, -um

15+

míser, mísera, míserum

15+

nam

15+

nec, néque
nec (néque)...nec (néque)

15+

nōn

15+

nóster, nóstra, nóstrum

15+

núllus, -a, -um

15+

nunc

15+

ómnis, -e

my, mine

mind

(dementia)

for

wretched, unhappy

(misery)

not; no

and not, and no, not, nor
neither…nor

(*non*-prefix: nonissue)

no, none, not; no one

our, ours

(nullify)

all, every

now

(omniscient)

15+

puélla, puéllae, *f.*

15+

-que
-que...-que

15+

quī, quae, quod

15+

quis, quid

15+

sed

15+

sī

15+

—, súī, síbi, sē (sḗsē), sē (sḗsē)

15+

sum, ésse, fúī, futū́rus

15+

tū, túī, tíbi, tē (tḗtē), tē (tḗtē)

15+

túus, -a, -um

and
both...and

girl; girlfriend

who, what; anyone, anything

who, which, that; any; what

if

but

to be; (with *male* or *maligne*) to go

(essence)

himself, herself, itself, themselves

your, yours (*s.*)

you (*s.*)

15+	15+
út (útī)	vídeō, -ére, vídī, vísus
15+	9-14
vólō, vélle, vóluī	ánimus, ánimī, *m.*
9-14	9-14
cor, córdis, *n.*	cum (*prep.*)
9-14	9-14
déus, déī, *m.*	dō, dáre, dédī, dátus
9-14	9-14
dúlcis, -e	férō, férre, túlī, lắtus

to see; (*pass.*) to be seen, seem

(providence, vision)

as, when; like; where;
how; so that, that

spirit; mind; heart

(animosity)

to wish, want; to like;
(taken with *bene*) to like

(benevolent)

(with *abl.*) with

(*com-*, *con-*prefixes: commit, convene)

heart; (*dat.*) dear, pleasing

(cordial)

to give; to pay

(dative)

god

(deification)

to bring, carry; to bear;
to support; to say

(transfer, relate)

sweet; dear, beloved

(dulcimer)

hómō, hóminis, *m.*

is, éa, id

lítus, lítoris, *n.*

mágnus, -a, -um

míttō, -ere, mísī, míssus

mors, mórtis, *f.*

múltus, -a, -um

mū́nus, mū́neris, *n.*

nōs, nóstrum (nóstrī), nṓbīs, nōs, nṓbīs

ō

this; that; he, she, it

person, human being

(homicide)

large, great

(magnify, magnanimous)

shore

(littoral)

death

(mortify)

to send; to let go, release; to utter

(remit, mission)

duty, tribute; gift; service

(remunerate)

much; (*pl.*) many

(*multi*-prefix: multinational)

oh

we, us

péctus, péctoris, *n.*

quam

quárē

quod

sīc

símul

síve

súus, -a, -um

tam

Théseus, Théseī, *m.*
(*acc.*: Thésea; *voc.*: Théseu)

how; than; (with *tam*) as;
(taken with *ante* or *prius*) before

chest; heart

(pectoral)

because; the fact that; (with *si*) but

for what reason, why; therefore

at the same time; together;
as soon as; (with *ac*) as soon

in this way, so, thus

(simultaneous)

his, her, its, their (own)

or, whether

(son of Aegeus)

so; (with *quam*) as

9-14

tŏtus, -a, -um

9-14

tum

9-14

únda, úndae, *f.*

9-14

űnus, -a, -um

9-14

-ve

9-14

vĭta, vĭtae, *f.*

5-8

accípiō, -ere, accḗpī, accéptus

5-8

Ácmē, Ácmēs, *f.* (*acc.:* Ácmēn)

5-8

aéquor, aéquoris, *n.*

5-8

aétās, aetătis, *f.*

then, at that moment;
(with *cum*) but also

all, whole, entire

(totalitarian)

one; alone, only

(unify)

wave; water

(undulate)

life

(vitality)

or

(Septimius' girlfriend)

to receive, accept; to hear

(acceptable)

age; lifetime; time

surface; water; sea

ágō, -ere, égī, áctus

ánte

aúra, aúrae, *f.* (archaic *abl.pl.*: aúreīs)

beắtus, -a, -um

béllus, -a, -um

béne

bónus, -a, -um

cándidus, -a, -um

cármen, cárminis, *n.*

cértē

(*adv.*) before, previously
(*prep.* with *acc.*) before, in front of

(antecedent)

to drive; to give (thanks);
to live (a life); to spend (time)

(agent, interaction)

happy, fortunate

(beatification)

breeze

well; quite

(*bene*-prefix: benefactor)

pretty, nice, charming

white; bright; radiant

(candid)

good

(bonafide)

certainly

(certitude)

song, poem

córpus, córporis, *n.*

crūdélis, -e

cū́ra, cū́rae, *f.*

dēlíciae, dēliciárum, *f.pl.*

déserō, -ere, dēséruī, dēsértus

dívus, dívī, *m.*

dólor, dolóris, *m.*

dómus, dómūs *or* dómī, *f.*

dum

ērípiō, -ere, ērípuī, ēréptus

savage, cruel

(cruelty)

body

(corporeal)

delight, pleasure;
darling, sweetheart

(delicious)

care, concern, worry

(curative)

god

(divine)

to desert, abandon

(desertion)

home, house

(domicile)

pain, grief

(doleful)

to snatch away; to rescue

while, as long as; until

5-8	5-8
extrḗmus, -a, -um	fáctum, fáctī, *n.*

5-8	5-8
fídēs, fídeī, *f.*	fíō, fíerī, fáctus sum

5-8	5-8
fortū́na, fortū́nae, *f.*	frā́ter, frā́tris, *m.*

5-8	5-8
fúgiō, -ere, fū́gī, fugitū́rus	fúror, furṓris, *m.*

5-8	5-8
gaúdeō, -ḗre, gavī́sus sum	gnā́tus, gnā́tī, *n.*

deed

(factory)

very remote; final, last; inmost

(extreme)

to be done; to be made; to happen

trust, belief, faith

(fidelity)

brother

(fraternal)

fortune

(unfortunate)

madness, frenzy; passion

(furious)

to flee

(refuge, fugitive)

son

(native)

to rejoice, take pleasure

(gaudy)

5-8

hábeō, -ére, -uī, -itus

5-8

heu

5-8

hīc

5-8

hūc

5-8

ídem, éadem, ídem

5-8

ímmemor, immémoris (*gen.*)

5-8

ínquam, — , ínquiī

5-8

íste, ísta, ístud

5-8

iūcúndus, -a, -um

5-8

Iúppiter, Ióvis, *m.*

alas

to have, hold, keep; to consider

(habitual)

(to) here, to this place

here, in this place, at this point

forgetful, unmindful

(memorial)

the same; likewise

(identity)

that (of yours), that (which you see);
he, she, it

to say

Jupiter (king of the gods);
weather, wind

(Jovial)

pleasant, delightful, pleasing

lábor, labóris, *m.*

Lésbia, Lésbiae, *f.*

línquō, -ere, líquī

línteum, línteī, *n.*

lóngus, -a, -um

lúctus, lúctūs, *m.*

lū́dō, -ere, lū́sī, lū́sus

lū́men, lū́minis, *n.*

maéstus, -a, -um

mále

(pseudonym of Catullus' lover)

labor, task; effort

(laborious)

napkin; sail

to leave

(relic, relinquish)

grief

long

(longitude)

light; eye

(illuminate)

to play, have fun

(ludicrous)

badly

(malefactor)

sad

5-8

málum, málī, *n.*

5-8

mā́ter, mā́tris, *f.*

5-8

mílle (*pl.*: mília)

5-8

módo

5-8

móllis, -e

5-8

-ne

5-8

nē

5-8

nēquíquam

5-8

níhil

5-8

nṓlō, nṓlle, nṓluī

mother

(maternal)

evil; misfortune; harm; distress

(malign)

only, just; now

thousand

(mile)

(enclitic interrogative particle)

soft, gentle

(mollify)

in vain, to no effect

so that not; that not; not;
(to negate the imperative) don't

to be unwilling, not want;
(*imper.*) don't

nothing

(annihilate)

nóvus, -a, -um

océllus, océllī, *m.*

ōs, ṓris, *n.*

párō, -ā́re, -ā́vī, -ā́tus

pásser, pásseris, *m.*

per (with *acc.*)

péreō, perī́re, périī, peritū́rus

pēs, pédis, *m.*

pétō, -ere, petī́vī, petī́tus

plūs, plū́ris (*gen.*)

little eye; jewel, darling

(binocular)

new

(novel)

to buy; to obtain

mouth; lip; face

(oral)

(with *acc.*) through, along

(*per*-prefix: perform)

sparrow

foot; leg (of a bed);
rope at lower part of a sail

(pedestrian)

to perish, die;
to be desperately in love

(perish)

more

(plurality)

to seek

(petition)

poéta, poétae, *m.*

pótis (póte)

prímum

príus

prō (with *abl.*)

pútō, -áre, -ávī, -átus

quális, -e

quántum

quísquam, quícquam

réddō, -ere, réddidī, rédditus

able, possible

(potent)

poet

(poetaster)

before, previously, earlier

first; (taken with *cum*) as soon as;
(taken with *quam*) as soon as possible

(primal)

to think

(reputation)

(with *abl.*) for, on behalf of; in return for

(*pro*-prefix: process)

whatever amount; as much as;
(with *tantus*) as

(quantity)

what (sort of); such as, like

(quality)

to give back, return; to deliver

(render)

anyone, anything

saépe

saévus, -a, -um

sǽnctus, -a, -um

sḗdēs, sḗdis, *f.*

seu

sṓlus, -a, -um

sub

tǽlis, -e

támen

tántum

savage

often

home

(sedimentary)

holy, sacred

(sanctimonious)

alone, only; lonely

(solitude)

or, whether; or if

such

(with *acc.* or *abl.*) under

(*sub*-prefix: subterranean)

such a great quantity; so; only;
(with *quantum*) as much

however, still, nevertheless

5-8 tántus, -a, -um	5-8 témpus, témporis, *n.*
5-8 téneō, -ére, -uī, téntus	5-8 úllus, -a, -um
5-8 úsque	5-8 váleō, -ére, -uī, -itúrus
5-8 véniō, -íre, vḗnī, ventúrus	5-8 véntus, véntī, *m.*
5-8 Vénus, Véneris, *f.*	5-8 venústus, -a, -um

time; need

(temporary)

such great, so great;
(with *quantus*) as great, as much

(tantamount)

any

to hold

(obtain, retention)

to be strong, be well; to prevail;
(*imper.*) goodbye

(valedictorian)

all the way; continuously

wind

(ventilation)

to come

(convention)

charming, attractive

(goddess of love); love, charm

5-8

saépe

5-8

saévus, -a, -um

5-8

sắnctus, -a, -um

5-8

sḗdēs, sḗdis, *f.*

5-8

seu

5-8

sṓlus, -a, -um

5-8

sub

5-8

tắlis, -e

5-8

támen

5-8

tántum

savage

often

home

(sedimentary)

holy, sacred

(sanctimonious)

alone, only; lonely

(solitude)

or, whether; or if

such

(with *acc.* or *abl.*) under

(*sub*-prefix: subterranean)

such a great quantity; so; only;
(with *quantum*) as much

however, still, nevertheless

5-8

tántus, -a, -um

5-8

témpus, témporis, *n.*

5-8

téneō, -ére, -uī, téntus

5-8

úllus, -a, -um

5-8

úsque

5-8

váleō, -ére, -uī, -itúrus

5-8

véniō, -íre, vḗnī, ventúrus

5-8

véntus, véntī, *m.*

5-8

Vénus, Véneris, *f.*

5-8

venústus, -a, -um

time; need

(temporary)

such great, so great;
(with *quantus*) as great, as much

(tantamount)

any

to hold

(obtain, retention)

to be strong, be well; to prevail;
(*imper.*) goodbye

(valedictorian)

all the way; continuously

wind

(ventilation)

to come

(convention)

charming, attractive

(goddess of love); love, charm

5-8

vĕrus, -a, -um

5-8

véstis, véstis, *f.*

5-8

vívō, -ere, víxī, vīctúrus

5-8

vōs, véstrum, vőbīs, vōs, vőbīs

5-8

vōx, vőcis, *f.*

garment, clothing; coverlet, bedspread

(vestibule)

true

(veracity)

you (*pl.*)

to live

(vivacious)

voice; word

(vocalize)

Meters of the Poems*

In English poetry metrical patterns are based on which syllables in a word are *stressed*, or said more emphatically. In Latin poetry, however, the metrical patterns are based on the *length* of the syllables in the Latin words, not on their stress. While the stress accent played some role in how Latin poetry sounded, the *length* of the syllables determined the particular meter being used in a given poem. For this reason the meters are called *quantitative meters*, that is, they are based on the length or *quantity* of the syllables. The student or teacher should consult the prosody or versification section in a basic Latin grammar or text for rules about determining syllable length, and, more generally, for rules about figuring out Latin meter.

The metrical patterns consist of arrangements of short syllables (∪) and long syllables (—). A syllable marked (X) is called *anceps* ("double-headed") and can be long or short. The final syllable of each verse is anceps. When pronounced, long syllables are said for a longer time than short ones.

The student should learn to write out the *scansion*, or the marking of the long and short syllables and ELISIONS, in the poems. (Students taking the Advanced Placement Latin Exam will be *required* to do this on the exam.) After gaining competence in writing out the scansion, the student should become familiar with the *sound* of the Latin poetry. The best way to accomplish this is to write out the scansion of a particular passage, e.g., about four lines that make sense as a metrical and grammatical unit, to practice reading it with the appropriate long and short syllables, ELISIONS etc., and then to *memorize* it. Having such a "chunk" of Latin in one's head or on one's lips is the best way to reinforce the particular metrical patterns.

The following meters occur in the poems in this text: Dactylic Hexameter, Elegiac Couplets, Choliambic (limping iambic), Sapphic, Iambic Senarius, Greater Asclepiadean, Hendecasyllabic.

Dactylic Hexameter

Poem 64 is composed in dactylic hexameter, the same meter used in Latin for Vergil's *Aeneid* and Ovid's *Metamorphoses*, and in Greek for Homer's *Iliad* and *Odyssey*.

There are six feet ("hex" is Greek for "six") in a line or verse of dactylic hexameter poetry. (A FOOT is the smallest metrical unit of verse with a given sequence and number of short and long syllables.) The first five feet are either dactyls (— ∪ ∪) or spondees (— —) or any combination

*This discussion is taken from *Writing Passion: A Catullus Reader,* by Ronnie Ancona (Wauconda, IL: Bolchazy-Carducci Publishers, 2004).

of these (i.e., the first FOOT could be a dactyl, the second a spondee etc.). A dactyl is one long syllable followed by two short syllables. A spondee is two long syllables. The sixth FOOT is treated as a spondee (— —), but the second syllable of the spondee is actually anceps (— X). The fifth FOOT is *usually* a dactyl.

This is the metrical pattern of the line:

$$\underset{\smile\smile}{-}\,-\,/\,-\,-\,/\,-\,-\,/\,-\,-\,/\,-\,-\,/\,-\,X$$

A CAESURA (//) is a pause or break between words within a FOOT. The major pause in the line, called the principal CAESURA, usually occurs after the first syllable of the third FOOT or after the first syllable of the fourth FOOT.

Poem 64, line 50

    haec vestis priscīs hominum variāta figūrīs

$$-\quad -/-\;-\;/-\;\,\smile\smile/-\quad \smile\smile/-\smile\smile/-X$$

Elegiac Couplets

The elegiac couplet consists of alternating lines of dactylic hexameter and pentameter. (See the description of the dactylic hexameter line above.) The pentameter line gets its name ("pent" is Greek for five) from the fact that it consists of two times 2 ½ feet of hexameter. There is a pause or DIAERESIS in between. The first half of the pentameter consists of two and a half feet of hexameter with the substitutions of dactyls and spondees allowed in the hexameter line.

The second half of the pentameter does not allow substitution and consists of two dactylic feet and a half FOOT. The "half" feet in the pentameter are always one long syllable.

hexameter:

$$\underset{\smile\smile}{-}\,-\,/\,-\,-\,/\,-\,-\,/\,-\,-\,/\,-\,-\,/\,-\,X$$

pentameter:

$$-\smile\smile-\smile\smile$$
$$-\,-\,-\,-\,-\,//\,-\,\smile\smile\,-\,\smile\smile\,X$$

Poem 76, lines 1–2

Sī qua recordantī benefacta priōra voluptās

— ∪ ∪/— — /— ∪∪/— ∪ ∪ /—∪ ∪/— X

est hominī, cum sē cōgitat esse pium,

— ∪ ∪/— — / —//—∪∪/—∪ ∪/ X

Choliambic (also called limping iambics or scazons)

This line consists of five iambs (∪—) followed by a trochee (—∪) or spondee(— —). The "limping" quality of the line comes from the switch after the iambs to a final FOOT that begins with a long syllable. The first and third feet can be spondees instead of iambs.

Ū — / ∪ — / Ū — / ∪ — / ∪ — / — X

Poem 8, line 1

Miser Catulle, dēsinās ineptīre,
∪ — / ∪ — /∪ — /∪— /∪—/—X

Sapphic

The following is the metrical pattern of the Sapphic STANZA. The pattern is written as four lines, although the fourth line originally may have been thought of as just a lengthening of the third line:

— ∪ — ∪̲ — // ∪∪ — ∪ — X

— ∪ — ∪̲ — // ∪∪ — ∪ — X

— ∪ — ∪̲ — // ∪∪ — ∪ — X

— ∪∪ — X

The DIAERESIS does not always occur in this spot.

Poem 51, line 1

> Ille mī pār esse deō vidētur,
> —∪— — —∪ ∪—∪— X

> ille, sī fās est, superāre dīvōs,
> —∪— — — ∪∪ —∪ — X

> quī sedens adversus identidem tē
> — ∪ — — —∪ ∪—∪— X

> spectat et audit
> — ∪ ∪ — X

Iambic Senarius

This is a pure iambic trimeter consisting of six iambs.

> ∪ — ∪ — ∪ — ∪ — ∪ — ∪ X

Poem 4, line 1

> Phasēlus ille, quem vidētis, hospitēs,
> ∪ —∪ —∪ — ∪ —∪ — ∪ X

Greater Asclepiadean

> — — —∪∪ — ‖ — ∪∪ — ‖ — ∪∪ —∪ X

Poem 30, line 3

> iam mē prōdere, iam nōn dubitās fallere, perfide?
> — — — ∪∪ —‖— ∪∪—‖—∪∪ —∪ X

Hendecasyllabic (or Phalaecean)

This metrical line has eleven syllables ("hendeca" is Greek for "eleven"). It is the most common meter in Catullus' poems.

Poem 5, line 1

Vīvāmus, mea Lesbia, atque amēmus,

Metrical Terms, Tropes or Figures of Thought, and Rhetorical Figures or Figures of Speech*

The following is a list of definitions for terms that are important for (1) meter and (2) the figurative use of language, whether a departure from the standard meaning of a word (a trope) or a departure from the standard order of words (a rhetorical figure). References in parentheses are to examples from the Catullus poems in the Advanced Placement syllabus.

ALLITERATION: repetition of the same sound, usually initial, in two or more words. The term usually applies to consonants. (Poem 35, line 14: **Dindymi dominam**)

ANAPHORA: repetition of a word or phrase, often at the beginning of successive clauses or phrases. (Poem 5, line 8: ***dein* mille altera, *dein* secunda centum**)

APOSTROPHE: a "turning away" to address an often absent person or PERSONIFIED thing for rhetorical effect. (Poem 3, line 16: **[o factum male! o miselle passer!]**)

ASSONANCE: repetition of a sound, usually in the middle or at the end of a word, in successive words. (Poem 5, line 1: **Viva*m*us, *m*ea Lesbia, atque a*m*e*m*us,**)

ASYNDETON: lack of a conjunction between words or clauses. (Poem 45, line 20: **amant amantur**)

CAESURA: pause or break between words within a metrical FOOT.

CHIASMUS: arrangement of words parallel in syntax with corresponding words reversed in an A B B A pattern like the Greek letter *chi* (X). (Poem 44, line 13: **gravēdō frīgida et frequens tussis**)

DIAERESIS: pause or break between words that coincides with the end of a metrical unit.

ECPHRASIS: literary description of an object. (Poem 64, lines 50 ff.: **Haec vestis...,** of the bedspread)

ELISION: suppression, partial suppression, or blending of a final syllable of a word ending in a vowel (or a vowel followed by the letter *m*) before another word beginning with a vowel (or the letter *h* followed by a vowel). ELISION is indicated in scansion by writing the symbol (◡) from the end of the first word to the beginning of the second word as well as by crossing through with a single line (/) or putting in parentheses () the elided letters.

ELLIPSIS: omission of a word or words that must be understood from the context. (Poem 84, line 2: **insidias Arrius hinsidias**)

FOOT: the smallest metrical unit of verse with a given sequence and number of short and long syllables.

*This discussion is taken from *Writing Passion: A Catullus Reader,* by Ronnie Ancona (Wauconda, IL: Bolchazy-Carducci Publishers, 2004).

GOLDEN LINE: two adjectives and two nouns with a verb between. (Poem 64, line 59: **irrita ventosae linquens promissa procellae**)

HENDIADYS: one idea expressed through two words joined by a copulative conjunction. (Poem 14a, line 8: **novum ac repertum**)

HIATUS: lack of ELISION. (Poem 3, line 16: **[o factum male! o miselle passer!]**)

HYPERBATON: disruption of normal prose word order, for example, through wide separation of noun and modifier. (Poem 44, line 9: **dedit**)

HYPERBOLE: extravagant exaggeration. (Poem 69: exaggerated description of bad odor)

HYPERMETRIC LINE: a line that has an extra syllable which must be ELIDED to the next line. (Poem 11, line 19: **omnium / ilia**)

HYSTERON PROTERON: reversal of natural or chronological order of events. (Poem 50, line 13: **loquerer...essem**)

IAMBIC SHORTENING: (An iamb is a short syllable followed by a long syllable.) According to this metrical law, a long syllable, if preceded by a short syllable, may be counted as short if the word's natural accent falls on the syllable directly preceding or following it. (Poem 13, line 11: **dabo**) Here, **dabo** ($\cup$ —) can become ($\cup\cup$) because the word is accented on the first syllable, i.e., the syllable preceding the change.

IRONY: statement in which implied meaning is different from explicitly stated meaning. (Poem 70, use of Jupiter as potential marital partner)

LITOTES: understatement, usually involving the assertion of something by denying its opposite. (Poem 4, lines 3–4: **neque...nequisse**)

METAPHOR: implied comparison in the form of an identity. The "tenor" is the subject to which the METAPHORIC language is applied, while the "vehicle" is the METAPHORIC language itself. (Poem 1, line 2: **arida...pumice expolitum,** where the idea of "polishing" is both literal and figurative or METAPHORICAL in terms of style)

METONYMY: application of a term for one thing to another with which it is closely associated. (Poem 64, line 67: **fluctus *salis* alludebant,** where "salt" is the "sea")

ONOMATOPOEIA: use of words which through their sound imitate their meaning. (Poem 64, line 155: **spumantibus exspuit**)

OXYMORON: paradox expressed through juxtaposition of seemingly contradictory words. (Poem 64, line 83: **funera... nec funera**)

PERSONIFICATION: application to inanimate objects of human qualities. (Poem 4: the speaking boat)

POSTPOSITION: placement of a word later than the location expected in prose; often, the placement of a word second rather than first in its clause. (Poem 51, line 5: **misero quod...**)

SIMILE: explicit comparison between two distinct things introduced by a word like **velut** (just as). (Poem 11, lines 22–23: **velut...flos**, of the speaker's love)

STANZA: division of a poem containing a series of lines repeating in a pattern.

SYNCHYSIS or INTERLOCKED WORD ORDER: arrangement of words parallel in syntax with an interlocking of the corresponding words in an A B A B pattern. (Poem 109, line 6: **aeternum hoc sanctae foedus amicitiae**.)

SYNCOPE: shortening of a form. (Poem 3, line 6: **norat**: syncopated form of **noverat)**

SYNECDOCHE: part of something used to signify the whole. (Poem 31, line 9: **larem**, for "home")

SYNIZESIS: the joining of two successive vowels within a word into one long syllable. (Poem 64, line 229: **Erectheī: -eī** one syllable)

TMESIS: separation of a compound word. (Poem 64, lines 91–92: **prius...quam**)

TRANSFERRED EPITHET (or HYPALLAGE): transfer of an adjective from the noun it goes with "in sense" to another related noun. (Poem 7, line 5: **aestuosi**)

TRICOLON CRESCENDO: arrangement of three phrases, clauses etc. with increasing length. (Poem 2, lines 2–4: **quicum ludere, quem in sinu tenere,/cui primum digitum dare appetenti**)

COMPLETE AP* CATULLUS VOCABULARY

(I have used *Vox Latina: A Guide to the Pronunciation of Classical Latin* by W. Sidney Allen to determine the length of vowels.)

A

ā ah

ā, ab (with *abl.*) from; by

abeō, abīre, abiī, abitūrus to go away, depart

abhorreō, -ēre, -uī to be different

absūmō, -ere, absūmpsī, absūmptus to exhaust; to kill

abūtor, -ī, abūsus sum (with *abl.*) to abuse

ac, atque and; as

acceptus, -a, -um welcome, pleasing

accidit, -ere, accidit to happen, develop

accipiō, -ere, accēpī, acceptus to receive, accept; to hear

ācer, ācris, ācre sharp; fierce

acerbus, -a, -um bitter

aciēs, aciēī, *f.* gaze, sight

Acmē, Acmēs, *f.* (*acc.*: **Acmēn**) (Septimius' girlfriend)

acquiēscō, -ere, acquiēvī to rest, relax

ad (with *acc.*) to; at; for

adeō, adīre, adiī, aditūrus to go to, approach

adimō, -ere, adēmī, adēmptus (with *dat.*) to take away from

admīror, -ārī, -ātus sum to wonder, be amazed

adveniō, -īre, advēnī, adventūrus to come, arrive

adventō, -āre, -āvī, -ātūrus to approach

adventus, adventūs, *m.* arrival

adversus, -a, -um opposite, facing

advocō, -āre, -āvī, -ātus to summon; to invoke

Aegeus, Aegeī, *m.* (legendary king of Athens, father of Theseus)

aequē equally

aequinoctiālis, -e equinoctial

aequō, -āre, -āvī, -ātus to smooth

aequor, aequoris, *n.* surface; water; sea

āereus, -a, -um airy; lofty

āerius, -a, -um airy; lofty

aes, aeris, *n.* bronze, money

aestimātiō, aestimātiōnis, *f.* value, worth

aestimō, -āre, -āvī, -ātus to appraise, value

aestuōsus, -a, -um hot, sultry

aestus, aestūs, *m.* tide, surge

aetās, aetātis, *f.* age; lifetime; time

aeternus, -a, -um eternal

aevum, aevī, *n.* time, age

afferō, afferre, attulī, allātus to bring

ager, agrī, *m.* field, land

agnōscō, -ere, agnōvī, agnitus to recognize

agō, -ere, ēgī, āctus to drive; to give (thanks); to live (a life); to spend (time)

ait (he, she, it) says

āla, ālae, *f.* armpit

āles, ālitis, *m.f.* bird

Alfēnus, Alfēnī, *m.* (false friend of Catullus)

alga, algae, *f.* seaweed

aliquī, aliqua, aliquod some

aliquis, aliquid someone, something

alius, alia, aliud other

alloquor, -ī, allocūtus sum to speak to, address

allūdō, -ere, allūsī to play, frolick

alluō, -ere, alluī to wash over

alō, -ere, aluī, altus to nourish

Alpēs, Alpium, *f.pl.* Alps

alter, altera, alterum a second, (an)other

altus, -a, -um high

amābilis, -e lovable

amāns, amantis, *m.f.* lover

amāritiēs, amāritiēī, *f.* bitterness

Amastris, Amastridis, *f.* (capital of Paphlagonia)

Amathūs, Amathuntis, *f.* (*acc.*: **Amathunta**) (town in Cyprus)

---

ambō, ambae, ambō both

āmēns, āmentis (*gen.*) insane

amīca, amīcae, *f.* girlfriend; mistress

amīcitia, amīcitiae, *f.* friendship

amictus, amictūs, *m.* garment, clothing

amīculus, amīculī, *m.* dear friend

amīcus, amīcī, *m.* friend

amitha / ācta (manuscript error usually read as ācta)

āmittō, -ere, āmīsī, āmissus to lose

amō, -āre, -āvī, -ātus to love

amor, amōris, *m.* love; lover; Cupid (god of love)

amplius more, further

an or

Ancōn, Ancōnis, *f.* (*acc.*: **Ancōna**) (seaport town in Picenum)

Androgeōnēus, -a, -um of Androgeos (son of Minos and Pasiphae)

anguīnus, -a, -um snaky

angustus, -a, -um narrow

anima, animae, *f.* soul, life

animus, animī, *m.* spirit; mind; heart

annālēs, annālium, *m.pl.* annals, chronicles

annuō, -ere, annuī to nod assent

annus, annī, *m.* year

ante (*adv.*) before, previously; (*prep. with acc.*) before, in front of

anteā previously, before

antenna, antennae, *f.* sail

Antius, Antī, *m.* (a candidate)

ānxius, -a, -um troubled, worried

apertus, -a, -um open

apīscor, -ī, aptus to get, attain

appāreō, -ēre, -uī, -itus to appear

appetō, -ere, appetīvī, appetītus to seek; to attack

approbātiō, approbātiōnis, *f.* approval

apud (with *acc.*) at the house of

aqua, aquae, *f.* water

Aquīnus, Aquīnī, *m.* (bad poet)

āra, ārae, *f.* altar

Arabs, Arabis, *m.* (*acc.pl.*: **Arabas**) Arab

arānea, arāneae, *f.* cobweb

arātrum, arātrī, *n.* plow

ārdeō, -ēre, ārsī to burn, blaze

ārdor, ārdōris, *m.* passion

Ariadna, Ariadnae, *f.* Ariadne (daughter of king Minos)

āridus, -a, -um dry

Arrius, Arrī, *m.* (social climber with affected speech)

ars, artis, *f.* skill, art

artus, artūs, *m.* limb

arx, arcis, *f.* citadel

as, assis, *m.* bronze coin of little value

Asia, Asiae, *f.* Asia Minor

Asinius, Asinī, *m.* (Asinius Marrucinus, napkin thief)

aspiciō, -ere, aspexī, aspectus to look, look at

assiduus, -a, -um constant

at but

Athēnae, Athēnārum, *f.pl.* Athens

attamen even so, nevertheless

attingō, -ere, attigī, attāctus to touch, undertake; to reach

attribuō, -ere, attribuī, attribūtus to assign

audāx, audācis (*gen.*) bold, presumptuous

audeō, -ēre, ausus sum to dare

audiō, -īre, -īvī, -ītus to hear, listen to

auferō, auferre, abstulī, ablātus to carry away, take away

augeō, -ēre, auxī, auctus to furnish

aura, aurae, *f.* (archaic *abl.pl.*: **aureīs**) breeze

Aurēlius, Aurēlī, *m.* (acquaintance of Catullus)

auris, auris, *f.* ear

aurum, aurī, *n.* gold

auspicātus, -a, -um lucky, auspicious

auspicium, auspicī, *n.* augury, omen

aut or, either

autem however, furthermore

autumō, -āre, -āvī, -ātus to say

auxilium, auxilī, *n.* help, aid

āvehō, -ere, āvexī, āvectus to carry away

aveō, -ēre to desire, yearn; (*imper.*) hail, greetings

avia, aviae, *f.* grandmother

avunculus, avunculī, *m.* maternal uncle

avus, avī, *m.* grandfather

B

bacchāns, bacchantis, *f.* bacchante (follower of Bacchus)

bāsiātiō, bāsiātiōnis, *f.* kiss

bāsiō, -āre, -āvī, -ātus to kiss

bāsium, bāsī, *n.* kiss

Battiadēs, Battiadae, *m.* inhabitant of Cyrene (here Callimachus)

Battus, Battī, *m.* (legendary founder of Cyrene)

beātus, -a, -um happy, fortunate

bellus, -a, -um pretty, nice, charming

bene well; quite

benefactum, benefactī, *n.* benefit, good deed

bēstia, bēstiae, *f.* beast

Bīthȳnia, Bīthȳniae, *f.* Bithynia (province in Asia Minor)

Bīthūnus, -a, -um Bithynian

blandus, -a, -um seductive

bonus, -a, -um good

brāchium, brāchī, *n.* arm; branch

brevis, -e short

Britannia, Britanniae, *f.* Britain

Britannus, Britannī, *m.* a Briton

buxifer, buxifera, buxiferum boxwood-bearing

C

cachinnus, cachinnī, *m.* loud laugh

cacō, -āre, -āvī, -ātus to defecate on

cacūmen, cacūminis, *n.* peak, top

cadō, -ere, cecidī, cāsūrus to fall

Caecilius, Caecilī, *m.* (love poet from Como)

caecus, -a, -um blind

caedēs, caedis, *f.* slaughter; blood

caelebs, caelibis (*gen.*) single

caeles, caelitis, *m.* god

caelestis, -e heavenly, celestial

caelicola, caelicolae, *m.f.* sky-dweller, god, goddess

caelum, caelī, *n.* sky

caeruleus, -a, -um blue

Caesar, Caesaris, *m.* (Gaius Julius Caesar)

caesius, -a, -um gray-eyed

Caesius, Caesī, *m.* (bad poet)

cālīgō, cālīginis, *f.* darkness

Calvus, Calvī, *m.* (Gaius Licinius Calvus Macer, Catullus' closest friend)

campus, campī, *m.* plain, field

candidus, -a, -um white; bright; radiant

cānitiēs, cānitiēī, *f.* gray hair

canō, -ere, cecinī, cantus to sing

caper, caprī, *m.* goat

capillus, capillī, *m.* hair

caprimulgus, caprimulgī, *m.* goat-milker

capsula, capsulae, *f.* small container (of scrolls)

caput, capitis, *n.* head

carbasus, carbasī, *f.* canvas, sail

carīna, carīnae, *f.* ship

carmen, carminis, *n.* song, poem

carpō, -ere, carpsī, carptus to consume

carta, cartae, *f.* (sheet or roll of) papyrus; volume

cārus, -a, -um dear, beloved

Carybdis, Carybdis, *f.* Charybdis (whirlpool between Italy and Sicily)

Castor, Castōris, *m.* (twin brother of Pollux)

castus, -a, -um pure, chaste

cāsus, cāsūs, *m.* misfortune; event

Catullus, Catullī, *m.* (Gaius Valerius Catullus, lyric poet)

caveō, -ēre, cāvī, cautus to beware, refrain from, watch out for

Cēcropia, Cēcropiae, *f.* Athens

Cēcropius, -a, -um Cecropian, Athenian

cēdō, -ere, cessī, cessūrus to depart

celer, celeris, celere swift, quick

cēlō, -āre, -āvī, -ātus to hide

cēna, cēnae, *f.* dinner

cēnō, -āre, -āvī, -ātus to dine

centum hundred

cernō, -ere, crēvī, crētus to see; to decide

certē certainly

ceu as

cibus, cibī, *m.* food

cieō, -ēre, cīvī, citus to produce

cinaedus, -a, -um shameless, crude

cingō, -ere, cīnxī, cīnctus to encircle

cinis, cineris, *m.f.* ashes

Cinna, Cinnae, *m.* (Gaius Helvius Cinna, neoteric poet)

circumsiliō, -īre to jump around

clārisonus, -a, -um clear-sounding

clārus, -a, -um famous

classis, classis, *f.* fleet, ship

clēmentia, clēmentiae, *f.* mercy

cliēns, clientis, *m.* client, dependent

Cnidus, Cnidī, *f.* (town in Asia Minor)

coetus, coetūs, *m.* crowd, band, company

cōgitātiō, cōgitātiōnis, *f.* thought

cōgitō, -āre, -āvī, -ātus to think

cognitus, -a, -um known, noted

cognōscō, -ere, cognōvī, cognitus to get to know

cōgō, -ere, coēgī, coāctus to drive; to compel, force

cohors, cohortis, *m.* staff (of a governor in a province)

colligō, -ere, collēgī, collēctus to collect

collis, collis, *m.* hill

collocō, -āre, -āvī, -ātus to set, place

collum, collī, *n.* neck

colō, -ere, coluī, cultus to inhabit

color, colōris, *m.* color

colōrō, -āre, -āvī, -ātus to color, stain

coma, comae, *f.* foliage

comātus, -a, -um leafy

comes, comitis, *m.f.* companion

commemorō, -āre, -āvī, -ātus to recall, relate

commodō, -āre, -āvī, -ātus to lend

commodum, commodī, *n.* opportunity; advantage

comparō, -āre, -āvī, -ātus to purchase; to compare

complector, -ī, complexus sum to embrace

complexus, complexūs, *m.* embrace

comprecor, -ārī, -ātus sum to beg, implore

Cōmum, Cōmī, *n.* (town in Cisalpine Gaul)

concēdō, -ere, concessī, concessūrus to yield, grant

concinō, -ere, concinuī to sing

concipiō, -ere, concēpī, conceptus to conceive

concrēdō, -ere, concrēdidī, concrēditus to entrust

concutiō, -ere, concussī, concussus to shake

condō, -ere, condidī, conditus to preserve

cōnficiō, -ere, cōnfēcī, cōnfectus to overcome, exhaust

cōnfiteor, -ērī, cōnfessus sum to admit

cōniger, cōnigera, cōnigerum cone-bearing

coniūnx, coniugis, *m.* husband

cōnor, -ārī, -ātus sum to try

conqueror, -ī, conquestus sum to complain

cōnsanguinea, cōnsanguineae, *f.* sister

cōnscendō, -ere, cōnscendī, cōnscēnsus to climb

cōnscius, -a, -um guilty

cōnscrībō, -ere, cōnscrīpsī, cōnscrīptus to write

cōnserō, -ere, cōnsēvī, cōnsitus to beset

cōnsilium, cōnsilī, *n.* plan

cōnsōlor, -ārī, -ātus sum to console

cōnspiciō, -ere, cōnspexī, cōnspectus to see

cōnstāns, cōnstantis (*gen.*) unchanging, constant

cōnsternō, -ere, cōnstrāvī, cōnstrātus to spread, cover

contegō, -ere, contēxī, contēctus to cover

contemptus, -a, -um vile, despicable

contendō, -ere, contendī, contentus to fight, contend

continuus, -a, -um next, following

contorqueō, -ēre, contorsī, contortus to whirl

contrā (*adv.*) in return; (*prep.* with *acc.*) against

contremō, -ere, contremuī to tremble

conturbō, -āre, -āvī, -ātus to mix up, confuse

cōnūbium, cōnūbī, *n.* marriage

convenit, -īre, convēnit to be agreed

convīva, convīvae, *m.* dinner guest

cōpia, cōpiae, *f.* supply, abundance

cor, cordis, *n.* heart; (*dat.*) dear, pleasing

Cornēlius, Cornēlī, *m.* (Cornelius Nepos, biographer and historian)

cornū, cornūs, *n.* horn

corpus, corporis, *n.* body

cortex, corticis, *m.* bark

crēdō, -ere, crēdidī, crēditus (with *dat.*) to believe; to entrust

creō, -āre, -āvī, -ātus to create

Crēta, Crētae, *f.* Crete

crūdēlis, -e savage, cruel

cubīle, cubīlis, *n.* bed

cubō, -āre, cubuī, cubitūrus to lie down

culpa, culpae, *f.* blame, fault

cum (*conj.*) when; since; although; (taken with *prīmum*) as soon as; (with *tum*) not only

cum (*prep.* with *abl.*) with

cūnctus, -a, -um all, whole

Cupīdō, Cupīdinis, *m.* Cupid (god of love); love, desire

cupidus, -a, -um longing, desiring, desirous

cupiō, -ere, cupīvī, cupītus to want, desire

cūr why; because of which

cūra, cūrae, *f.* care, concern, worry

cūriōsus, cūriōsī, *m.* busybody

cūrō, -āre, -āvī, -ātus to care, care for

currō, -ere, cucurrī, cursūrus to run

curvus, -a, -um curved

Cȳcladēs, Cȳcladum, *f.pl.* (islands in the Aegean surrounding Delos)

Cyrēnae, Cyrēnārum, *f.pl.* Cyrene (capital of Libya)

Cytōrius, -a, -um of Mount Cytorus

Cytōrus, Cytōrī, *m.* (mountain in Paphlagonia)

D

daps, dapis, *f.* sacrificial meal

Daulias, Dauliados (*gen.*) Daulian, of Daulis (town in Phocis)

dē (with *abl.*) from

dea, deae, *f.* goddess

decem ten

decet, -ēre, -uit to be suitable for, be appropriate for

dēclīnō, -āre, -āvī, -ātus to turn away

dēcoctor, dēcoctōris, *m.* bankrupt person

dēcursus, dēcursūs, *m.* downward course

decus, decoris, *n.* glory

dēdicō, -āre, -āvī, -ātus to dedicate

dēfendō, -ere, dēfendī, dēfēnsus to defend, protect

dēferō, dēferre, dētulī, dēlātus to carry down, bring down; to offer, confer

dēfessus, -a, -um tired

dein then, next

deinde then, next

dēlābor, -ī, dēlāpsus sum to slip down

dēlicātus, -a, -um self-indulgent; frivolous

dēliciae, dēliciārum, *f.pl.* delight, pleasure; darling, sweetheart

dēmānō, -āre, -āvī to flow down

dēnique finally

dēnsus, -a, -um thick, dense

dēperdō, -ere, dēperdidī, dēperditus to ruin, destroy

dēpereō, -īre, dēperiī to be desperately in love with

dēpōnō, -ere, dēposuī, dēpositus to lay aside, abandon

dēprecor, -ārī, -ātus sum to pray to prevent; to seek to avoid

dērigō, -ere, dērēxī, dērēctus to rule

dēserō, -ere, dēseruī, dēsertus to desert, abandon

dēsīderium, dēsīderī, n. desire; darling

dēsīderō, -āre, -āvī, -ātus to desire, long for

dēsinō, -ere, dēsiī, dēsitūrus to cease, stop

dēspuō, -ere to reject

dēstinātus, -a, -um stubborn, obstinate

dēsum, dē(e)esse, dēfuī (with *dat.*) to fail, neglect

deus, deī, m. god

dēvinciō, -īre, dēvīnxī, dēvīnctus to bind

dēvorō, -āre, -āvī, -ātus to eat up, devour

dēvoveō, -ēre, dēvōvī, dēvōtus to curse

dexter, dextera, dexterum right

dextra, dextrae, f. right side; right hand

Dīa, Dīae, f. (island in the Aegean Sea)

dicāx, dicācis (*gen.*) well-spoken, witty

dicō, -āre, -āvī, -ātus to show, indicate

dīcō, -ere, dīxī, dictus to say, tell; to call

dictum, dictī, n. word

diēs, diēī, m.f. day

differtus, -a, -um (with *gen.*) filled with, stuffed with

difficilis, -e difficult

digitus, digitī, m. finger

dīgredior, -ī, dīgressus sum to digress

dīlacerō, -āre, -āvī, -ātus to tear to pieces

dīligō, -ere, dīlēxī, dīlēctus to cherish, love

dīmittō, -ere, dīmīsī, dīmissus to send away, dismiss

Dindymus, Dindymī, m. (mountain in Phrygia sacred to Cybele)

dīrus, -a, -um terrible, awful

discēdō, -ere, discessī, discessūrus to depart

discernō, -ere, discrēvī, discrētus to separate

discerpō, -ere, discerpsī, discerptus to tear to pieces

disertus, -a, -um skilled in speaking, articulate

dispereō, -īre, disperiī to be destroyed

distīnctus, -a, -um different

dīva, dīvae, f. goddess

dīversus, -a, -um from different directions, different

dīvidō, -ere, dīvīsī, dīvīsus to divide

dīvus, dīvī, m. god

dō, dare, dedī, datus to give; to pay

doctus, -a, -um learned, scholarly

doleō, -ēre, -uī, -itūrus to suffer pain, grieve

dolor, dolōris, m. pain, grief

domina, dominae, f. mistress

dominus, dominī, m. master

domō, -āre, domuī, domitus to subdue, conquer

domus, domūs or **domī, f.** home, house

dōnō, -āre, -āvī, -ātus to give; to present, bestow

dōnum, dōnī, n. gift

dormiō, -īre, -īvī, -ītus to sleep

dubitō, -āre, -āvī, -ātūrus to hesitate

dubius, -a, -um uncertain

dūcō, -ere, dūxī, ductus to lead, take; to consider

dulce sweetly

dulcis, -e sweet; dear, beloved

dum while, as long as; until

Durrachium, Durrachī, n. Dyrrachium (town on the coast of Illyria)

dūrus, -a, -um hard, harsh

E

ē, ex (with *abl.*) out of, from

ēbrius, -a, -um drunk

edō, -ere, ēdī, ēsus to eat, eat away, consume

ēdō, -ere, ēdidī, ēditus to bring forth, produce

ēdūcō, -ere, ēdūxī, ēductus to bring out, produce

efficiō, -ere, effēcī, effectus to make, bring about

effigiēs, effigiēī, *f.* image, statue

effluō, -ere, efflūxī to flow out

ēgelidus, -a, -um unchilled, warm

ego, meī, mihi (mī), mē, mē I, me

ēgredior, -ī, ēgressus sum to go out

ēgressus, ēgressūs, *m.* departure

ēheu alas

ei alas

ēiciō, -ere, ēiēcī, ēiectus to cast ashore

ēlēctus, -a, -um select, choice

ēlegāns, ēlegantis (*gen.*) tasteful, refined, elegant

ēligō, -ere, ēlēgī, ēlēctus to choose

enim for

eō, īre, iī, itūrus to go

Eōus, -a, -um of the dawn; Eastern

epistolium, epistolī, *n.* short letter

Erecthēus, Erecthēī, *m.* (legendary king of Athens)

Erecthēus, -a, -um of Erectheus, Athenian

ēripiō, -ere, ēripuī, ēreptus to snatch away; to rescue

errābundus, -a, -um wandering

error, errōris, *m.* mistake; maze

ēruō, -ere, ēruī, ērutus to uproot

erus, erī, *m.* master

Erycīna, Erycīnae, *f.* (cult title of Venus)

et and, both; even

etiam also, even

etsī although

Eumenidēs, Eumenidum, *f.pl.* Furies

Eurōtās, Eurōtae, *m.* (river running through Sparta)

ēvītō, -āre, -āvī, -ātus to avoid

exagitō, -āre, -āvī, -ātus to rouse, stir up

exārdēscō, -ere, exārsī, exārsus to catch fire

exciō, -īre, -īvī, -itus to rouse

excitō, -āre, -āvī, -ātus to rouse

excruciō, -āre, -āvī, -ātus to torture, torment

excutiō, -ere, excussī, excussus to shake out

expallēscō, -ere, expalluī to turn pale

expellō, -ere, expulī, expulsus to drive, drive out

explicō, -āre, -āvī, -ātus to unfold, explain

expoliō, -īre, -īvī, -ītus to smooth, polish

exposcō, -ere, expoposcī to demand

exprimō, -ere, expressī, expressus to translate

exprōmō, -ere, exprōmpsī, exprōmptus to bring forth

exsolvō, -ere, exsolvī, exsolūtus to pay

exspectō, -āre, -āvī, -ātus to expect, wait for

exspīrō, -āre, -āvī, -ātus to breathe out; to emit

exspuō, -ere, exspuī, exspūtus to spit out

exsultō, -āre, -āvī to rejoice, revel

externō, -āre, -āvī, -ātus to terrify

extrēmus, -a, -um very remote; final, last; inmost

exturbō, -āre, -āvī, -ātus to drive out, banish

F

fābula, fābulae, *f.* story

Fabullus, Fabullī, *m.* (giver of napkins, colleague of Veranius)

facētiae, facētiārum, *f.pl.* cleverness, wit

faciō, -ere, fēcī, factus to do; to make; to write; to see to it; to value; to regard; to find

factum, factī, *n.* deed

fallāx, fallācis (*gen.*) deceitful, treacherous

fallō, -ere, fefellī, falsus to deceive, trick

falsus, -a, -um deceitful

famulor, -ārī, -ātus sum (with *dat.*) to serve

fās (*indecl.*) *n.* divine law, proper

fascinō, -āre, -āvī, -ātus to bewitch, jinx

fātum, fātī, *n.* fate

faveō, -ēre, fāvī, fautūrus (with *dat.*) to favor

fēmina, fēminae, *f.* woman

femur, femoris, *n.* thigh

fera, ferae, *f.* wild animal

ferō, ferre, tulī, lātus to bring, carry; to bear; to support; to say

ferōx, ferōcis (*gen.*) fierce

ferrūgō, ferrūginis, *f.* rust

ferus, -a, -um wild, uncivilized

fervidus, -a, -um fiery, hot

fessus, -a, -um tired

fētus, fētūs, *m.* offspring

fidēlis, -e faithful, reliable

fidēs, fideī, *f.* trust, belief, faith

fīdus, -a, -um faithful

fīgō, -ere, fīxī, fīxus to pierce

figūra, figūrae, *f.* figure

fīlia, fīliae, *f.* daughter

fīlum, fīlī, *n.* thread, string

fīnis, fīnis, *m.(f.)* end

fīō, fierī, factus sum to be done; to be made; to happen

flagrō, -āre, -āvī, -ātus to blaze

flāmen, flāminis, *n.* blast, wind, breeze

flamma, flammae, *f.* flame, fire

flāvus, -a, -um blonde

flectō, -ere, flexī, flexus to change

fleō, flēre, flēvī, flētus to weep, weep for, mourn

flētus, flētūs, *m.* weeping, tears

flexus, flexūs, *m.* turn, winding

flōreō, -ēre, -uī to bloom; to flourish

flōridus, -a, -um flowery

flōs, flōris, *m.* flower

flūctuō, -āre, -āvī, -ātus to waver

flūctus, flūctūs, *m.* wave

fluentisonus, -a, -um wave-resounding

fluitō, -āre, -āvī to flow

flūmen, flūminis, *n.* river

foedō, -āre, -āvī, -ātus to stain

foedus, foederis, *n.* agreement, treaty, compact

fōrma, fōrmae, *f.* shape, form, beauty

Fōrmiānus, -a, -um Formian, of Formiae (ancient city in south Latium)

fōrmōsus, -a, -um beautiful

fors, fortis, *f.* chance, luck

fortasse perhaps

forte by chance

fortūna, fortūnae, *f.* fortune

forum, forī, *n.* public square, Forum

fossor, fossōris, *m.* ditchdigger

frangō, -ere, frēgī, frāctus to break

frāter, frātris, *m.* brother

frāternus, -a, -um of a brother, brother's

frequēns, frequentis (*gen.*) constant, frequent

fretum, fretī, *n.* sea

frīgidulus, -a, -um cold

frīgidus, -a, -um chilly, cold

frīgus, frīgoris, *n.* chill, cold

frondōsus, -a, -um leafy

frōns, frontis, *f.* forehead

frūstrā in vain

frūstror, -ārī, -ātus sum to elude, evade

fuga, fugae, *f.* flight

fugiō, -ere, fūgī, fugitūrus to flee

fugō, -āre, -āvī, -ātus to drive away

fulgeō, -ēre, fulsī to shine, gleam

fulgor, fulgōris, *m.* glitter, gleam

funditus completely

fundō, -ere, fūdī, fūsus to pour

fundus, fundī, *m.* farm, country estate

fūnestō, -āre, -āvī, -ātus to pollute with death

fūnestus, -a, -um mournful

fūnis, fūnis, *m.* rope

fūnus, fūneris, *n.* death

Fūrius, Fūrī, *m.* (acquaintance of Catullus)

furō, -ere to rage

furor, furōris, *m.* madness, frenzy; passion

fūrtīvus, -a, -um secret

fūrtum, fūrtī, *n.* theft

G

Gaius, Gaī, *m.* (Gaius Helvius Cinna, neoteric poet)

Gallicus, -a, -um Gallic

gaudeō, -ēre, gavīsus sum to rejoice, take pleasure

gaudium, gaudī, *n.* joy

Gellius, Gellī, *m.* (Lucius Gellius Poplicola, rival of Catullus for Lesbia's love)

gemellus, gemellī, *m.* twin

geminus, -a, -um double, twin

gemō, -ere, gemuī, gemitus to lament

gener, generī, *m.* son-in-law

genitor, genitōris, *m.* father

gēns, gentis, *f.* nation, people

genus, generis, *n.* race

germānus, germānī, *m.* brother

gerō, -ere, gessī, gestus to carry, bear

gestiō, -īre, -īvī to exult, be cheerful

gignō, -ere, genuī, genitus to produce, give birth to

gnāta, gnātae, *f.* daughter

gnātus, gnātī, *n.* son

Gnōsius, -a, -um of Cnossos; Cretan

Golgī, Golgōrum, *m.pl.* (town in Cyprus noted for the worship of Venus)

Gortӯnius, -a, -um Gortynian, of Gortyna (a city in Crete); Cretan

grabātus, grabātī, *m.* cot, little bed

gradior, -ī, gressus sum to step, walk

grātēs, grātium, *f.pl.* thanks

grātiae, grātiārum, *f.pl.* thanks

grātus, -a, -um pleasing, welcome

gravēdō, gravēdinis, *f.* head cold

gravis, -e heavy, serious

gremium, gremī, *n.* lap

gurges, gurgitis, *m.* water

H

habeō, -ēre, -uī, -itus to have, hold, keep; to consider

habitō, -āre, -āvī, -ātus to live

Hadria, Hadriae, *f.* Adriatic Sea

Hadriāticum, Hadriāticī, *n.* Adriatic Sea

harēna, harēnae, *f.* sand; beach

harundinōsus, -a, -um reedy

hendecasyllabus, hendecasyllabī, *m.* hendecasyllabic verse (eleven syllable verse of poetry)

hērōs, hērōis, *m.* hero

hesternus, -a, -um yester-

heu alas

Hibērī, Hibērōrum, *m.pl.* Iberians, Spaniards

Hibērus, -a, -um Spanish

hic, haec, hoc this; he, she, it

hīc here, in this place, at this point

hinc from here

homō, hominis, *m.* person, human being

hōra, hōrae, *f.* hour

horreō, -ēre, -uī to shudder at

horribilis, -e terrifying, rough

horridus, -a, -um rough, harsh, dreadful

hospes, hospitis, *m.* guest, visitor, stranger

hūc (to) here, to this place

hymenaeī, hymenaeōrum, *m.pl.* wedding, marriage

Hyrcānī, Hyrcānōrum, *m.pl.* Hyrcanians (living on the Caspian shores)

I

Iacchus, Iacchī, *m.* (another name for Bacchus)

iaceō, -ēre, -uī, -itūrus to lie, recline

iaciō, -ere, iēcī, iactus to throw

iactō, -āre, -āvī, -ātus to toss

iam now, already; (with a negative) longer

iambus, iambī, *m.* iambic poem, lampoon

ibi there, then

Īdaeus, -a, -um of Mount Ida (on Crete)

Īdalium, Īdalī, *n.* (town in Cyprus sacred to Venus)

īdem, eadem, idem the same; likewise

identidem repeatedly, continually

igitur therefore

ignārus, -a, -um unaware

ignis, ignis, *m.* fire; flame (of passion)

ignōscō, -ere, ignōvī, ignōtus (with *dat.*) to forgive; to pardon

ignōtus, -a, -um unknown

īlia, īlium, *n.pl.* groin, genitals

ille, illa, illud that; he, she, it

illepidus, -a, -um uncharming; unrefined

illic, illaec, illuc that

illīc there, in that place

illinc from there

illūc there, to that place

imbuō, -ere, imbuī, imbūtus to dip, wet

immātūrus, -a, -um untimely

immemor, immemoris (*gen.*) forgetful, unmindful

immītis, -e harsh, bitter

immō on the contrary

impēnsus, -a, -um great, vehement

impetus, impetūs, *m.* rapid motion

impius, -a, -um disrespectful; wicked

impotēns (inpotēns), impotentis (*gen.*) powerless; uncontrollable

īmus, -a, -um deepest; bottom of

in (with *acc.*) into; upon, to; against; among; (with *abl.*) in, on, among; at; for

incendium, incendī, *n.* fire

incendō, -ere, incendī, incēnsus to burn, inflame

incidō, -ere, incidī, incāsūrus to fall (on); (with *dat.*) to fall upon

incitō, -āre, -āvī, -ātus to incite, provoke

incohō, -āre, -āvī, -ātus to begin

incola, incolae, *m.f.* inhabitant

incommodum, incommodī, *n.* trouble; misfortune

incurvō, -āre, -āvī, -ātus to bend

inde from there, from that point, then

India, Indiae, *f.* (country extending from the Indus river to China)

indicō, -āre, -āvī, -ātus to show, declare

indignē undeservedly

indomitus, -a, -um wild; untamed; uncontrollable

indūcō, -ere, indūxī, inductus to lead (into)

Indus, Indī, *m.* Indian (inhabitant of India)

ineptiō, -īre to play the fool

ineptus, -a, -um foolish

īnfacētus, -a, -um crude, witless

īnfēlīx, īnfēlīcis (*gen.*) unlucky

īnferiae, īnferiārum, *f.pl.* last rites

īnfestus, -a, -um dangerous; hostile

īnficētiae, īnficētiārum, *f.pl.* unrefinement

īnficiō, -ere, īnfēcī, īnfectus to dye

īnfimus, -a, -um lowest

īnfundō, -ere, īnfūdī, īnfūsus to pour on

ingenuus, -a, -um noble

ingrātus, -a, -um unpleasant; ungrateful unappreciated

ingredior, -ī, ingressus sum to enter

inguen, inguinis, *n.* groin

iniciō, -ere, iniēcī, iniectus (iniactus) to thow on; to throw (*acc.*) around (*dat.*)

inīquus, -a, -um unfair; treacherous

iniūria, iniūriae, *f.* wrongdoing, injustice

iniūstus, -a, -um unfair, unjust

inmerēns, inmerentis (*gen.*) undeserving

innūpta, innūptae, *f.* unmarried girl, maiden

inobservābilis, -e untraceable

inops, inopis (*gen.*) helpless

inquam, — , inquiī to say

īnsapiēns, īnsapientis (*gen.*) unwise, foolish

īnsidiae, īnsidiārum, *f.pl.* ambush, plot

īnsula, īnsulae, *f.* island

īnsulsus, -a, -um witless, stupid

īnsultō, -āre, -āvī, -ātus to mock

inter (with *acc.*) between, among

intereā meanwhile

interficiō, -ere, interfēcī, interfectus to destroy, kill

interior, interius inner

interitus, interitūs, *m.* death

intestīna, intestīnōrum, *n.pl.* guts

intorqueō, -ēre, intorsī, intortus to twist

invenustus, -a, -um ungraceful, unattractive

invictus, -a, -um invincible

invideō, -ēre, invīdī, invīsus to envy; to begrudge

invīsō, -ere, invīsī, invīsus to look upon, see

invītus, -a, -um unwilling

iocor, -ārī, -ātus sum to say in jest

iocōsus, -a, -um humorous; playful

iocus, iocī, *m.* joke, jest

Īonius, -a, -um of the Ionian Sea, Ionian

ipse, ipsa, ipsum -self; (*f.*) mistress

īra, īrae, *f.* anger, wrath

irritus, -a, -um worthless, useless

irrumātor, irrumātōris, *m.* vile person

is, ea, id this; that; he, she, it

iste, ista, istud that (of yours), that (which you see); he, she, it

istinc from there

ita thus, so, in this way

Italī, Italōrum, *m.pl.* Italians

iter, itineris, *n.* journey; path; course

Itōnus, Itōnī, *m.* (Thessalian or Boeotian town having cults of Athena)

Itylus, Itylī, *m.* (son of Procne and Tereus)

iubeō, -ēre, iussī, iussus to order

iūcundus, -a, -um pleasant, delightful, pleasing

iugum, iugī, *n.* ridge (of a mountain)

Iuppiter, Iovis, *m.* Jupiter (king of the gods); weather, wind

iūrō, -āre, -āvī, -ātus to swear, take an oath

iūstus, -a, -um just

iuvenis, iuvenis, *m.* youth, young man

iuvō, -āre, iūvī, iūtus to help; to please

L

labefactō, -āre, -āvī, -ātus to weaken

labellum, labellī, *n.* little lip

labor, labōris, *m.* labor, task, effort

labōriōsus, -a, -um industrious, much worked upon

labyrinthēus, -a, -um labyrinthine

lacrima, lacrimae, *f.* tear(drop)

lactēns, lactentis (*gen.*) milk-white

lacus, lacūs, *m.* lake

laedō, -ere, laesī, laesus to injure, offend

laetitia, laetitiae, *f.* happiness, joy

laetor, -ārī, -ātus sum to rejoice, delight

laetus, -a, -um happy

laevus, -a, -um left

languēns, languentis (*gen.*) faint, weak

languēscō, -ere, languī to grow weak

languidus, -a, -um sluggish, slow

lapis, lapidis, *m.* precious stone, jewel

lār, laris, *m.* household god; house, home

Lārius, -a, -um of Lake Larius (in Cisalpine Gaul)

lāsarpīcifer, -fera, -ferum silphium-producing

lātrō, -āre, -āvī, -ātus to bark

lātus, -a, -um wide

laus, laudis, *f.* praise

leaena, leaenae, *f.* lioness

lectīca, lectīcae, *f.* litter

lectulus, lectulī, *m.* little bed, little couch

lectus, lectī, *m.* bed, couch

legō, -ere, lēgī, lēctus to read

lēniō, -īre, -īvī, -ītus to appease, calm

lēnis, -e soft, gentle

lentus, -a, -um flexible, pliable

leō, leōnis, *m.* lion

lepidus, -a, -um charming; witty

lepōs, lepōris, *m.* charm, grace, wit

Lesbia, Lesbiae, *f.* (pseudonym of Catullus' lover)

Lēthaeus, -a, -um of Lethe (underworld river of forgetfulness)

lētum, lētī, *n.* death

levis, -e light

leviter lightly, slightly, a little

levō, -āre, -āvī, -ātus to lighten

libellus, libellī, *m.* little book

libenter gladly, willingly

liber, librī, *m.* book

līber, lībera, līberum free

libīdō, libīdinis, *f.* desire, lust

librārius, librārī, *m.* bookseller

Libya, Libyae, *f.* North Africa

Libyssus, -a, -um North African

Libystīnus, -a, -um North African

licet, -ēre, -uit to be permitted

Licinius, Licinī, *m.* (Gaius Licinius Macer Calvus, friend of Catullus)

lignum, lignī, *n.* wood, firewood

līmen, līminis, *n.* threshold

limpidus, -a, -um clear, transparent

lingua, linguae, *f.* tongue

linquō, -ere, līquī to leave

linteum, linteī, *n.* napkin; sail

liquēns, liquentis (*gen.*) clear

liquidus, -a, -um clear

lītorālis, -e of the shore

litterātor, litterātōris, *m.* schoolmaster

lītus, lītoris, *n.* shore

locō, -āre, -āvī, -ātus to place

longē far; by far

longus, -a, -um long

loquor, -ī, locūtus sum to speak, talk; to say, tell

lōrum, lōrī, *n.* leather strap

lubet, -ēre (with *dat.*) to be pleasing

lūceō, -ēre, lūxī to be light

lūctus, lūctūs, *m.* grief

lūdō, -ere, lūsī, lūsus to play, have fun

lūgeō, -ēre, lūxī, lūctus to mourn

lūmen, lūminis, *n.* light; eye

lūx, lūcis, *f.* light; day

Lȳdius, -a, -um Lydian, of Lydia (country in Asia Minor)

lympha, lymphae, *f.* water

M

maeror, maerōris, *m.* grief, mourning

maestus, -a, -um sad

magis more; rather

magnanimus, -a, -um brave, bold

magnus, -a, -um large, great

male badly

malignē badly, poorly

malignus, -a, -um spiteful, malicious

mālō, mālle, māluī to prefer

malum, malī, *n.* evil; misfortune; harm; distress

mālum, mālī, *n.* apple

malus, -a, -um bad, evil

mālus, mālī, *m.* mast

mandātum, mandātī, *n.* order, command

maneō, -ēre, mānsī, mānsūrus to remain, stay; to wait; to endure

Mānius, Mānī, *m.* (Roman praenomen)

mānō, -āre, -āvī, -ātūrus to flow, drip

mantica, manticae, *f.* knapsack

manus, manūs, *f.* hand

Mārcus, Mārcī, *m.* (Marcus Tullius Cicero, orator and politician)

mare, maris, *n.* sea

Marrūcīnus, Marrūcīnī, *m.* (Asinius Marrucinus, napkin thief)

māter, mātris, *f.* mother

māternus, -a, -um maternal

medius, -a, -um middle of

medulla, medullae, *f.* marrow; heart

mellītus, -a, -um honey-sweet

membrānae, membrānārum, *f.pl.* parchment cover

membrum, membrī, *n.* limb

meminī, meminisse (*perf.* forms with *pres.* force) to remember

memor, memoris (*gen.*) mindful

mēns, mentis, *f.* mind

mersō, -āre, -āvī, -ātus to dip, immerse

merus, -a, -um pure, undiluted

-met (enclitic intensifier)

metuō, -ere, metuī to fear, be afraid of

meus, -a, -um my, mine

mīca, mīcae, *f.* particle, grain

micō, -āre, micuī to flash

mīliēs a thousand times

mīlle (*pl.:* **mīlia**) thousand

mināx, minācis (*gen.*) menacing, threatening

Mīnōis, Mīnōidis, *m.* daughter of Minos, Ariadne

Mīnōs, Mīnōis, *m.* (*acc.:* **Mīnōa**) (king of Crete, husband of Pasiphae)

Mīnōtaurus, Mīnōtaurī, *m.* Minotaur

minus less

mīrificē wonderfully, amazingly

mīror, -ārī, -ātus sum to admire

mīrum, mīrī, *n.* wonder

mīrus, -a, -um wonderful

misceō, -ēre, -uī, mixtus to mix

misellus, -a, -um poor little; wretched

miser, misera, miserum wretched, unhappy

misereor, -ērī, -itus sum to feel pity, feel compassion

miserēscō, -ere (with *gen.*) to pity

miseret, -ēre, -uit to feel pity: (*acc.*) feel pity for (*gen.*)

mitra, mitrae, *f.* (oriental) headdress (fastened with ribbons under the chin)

mittō, -ere, mīsī, missus to send; to let go, release; to utter

mnēmosynum, mnēmosynī, *n.* souvenir

modo only, just; now

modus, modī, *m.* way, method

moechus, moechī, *m.* adulterer

moenia, moenium, *n.pl.* city walls

molestus, -a, -um troublesome, annoying

mollis, -e soft, gentle

monimentum, monimentī, *n.* memorial, monument

mōns, montis, *m.* mountain

mōnstrum, mōnstrī, *n.* monster

morbus, morbī, *m.* disease

mordeō, -ēre, momordī, morsus to bite

morior, -ī, mortuus sum to die

moror, -ārī, -ātus sum to delay, linger

mors, mortis, *f.* death

morsus, morsūs, *m.* bite

mortālis, -e mortal

mortuus, -a, -um dead

mōs, mōris, *m.* custom, practice

mōtus, mōtūs, *m.* motion

moveō, -ēre, mōvī, mōtus to move

mulier, mulieris, *f.* woman

multa, multae, *f.* penalty

multiplex, multiplicis (*gen.*) varied

multō (by) much

multō, -āre, -āvī, -ātus to punish

multum a lot, much

multus, -a, -um much; (*pl.*) many

mundus, mundī, *m.* universe

mūnus, mūneris, *n.* duty, tribute; gift; service

mūnusculum, mūnusculī, *n.* little gift

mūsa, mūsae, *f.* muse

mūtō, -āre, -āvī, -ātus to change; to exchange

mūtus, -a, -um mute, silent

mūtuus, -a, -um mutual, reciprocal

myrtus, myrtī, *f.* (*nom.pl. & acc.pl.:* **myrtūs**) myrtle (tree)

N

nam for

namque for

nārrō, -āre, -āvī, -ātus to tell; to say

nāscor, -ī, nātus sum to be born; to develop

nāsus, nāsī, *m.* nose

natō, -āre, -āvī, -ātūrus to float, swim

naufragus, -a, -um shipwrecked

nāvis, nāvis, *f.* ship

nāvita, nāvitae, *m.* sailor

-ne (enclitic interrogative particle)

nē so that not; that not; not; (to negate the imperative) don't

nebula, nebulae, *f.* cloud

nec, neque and not, and no, not, nor, neither

necdum and not yet

necesse necessary

nefārius, -a, -um evil, horrible

neglegēns, neglegentis (*gen.*) careless

neglegō, -ere, neglēxī, neglēctus to neglect, disregard

negō, -āre, -āvī, -ātus to deny; to say...not

Nemesis, Nemeseōs, *f.* (goddess of retribution)

nepōs, nepōtis, *m.* descendant

Neptūnus, Neptūnī, *m.* Neptune (god of the sea)

nequeō, nequīre, nequīvī to be unable

nēquīquam in vain, to no effect

nesciō, -īre, -īvī, -ītus not to know

nescio quis, nescio quid someone or other, something or other

nescius, -a, -um unaware

neu and so that...not

nī unless, if...not

Nīcaea, Nīcaeae, *f.* (city in Bithynia)

niger, nigra, nigrum dark, black

nihil nothing

nīl nothing; no, not

Nīlus, Nīlī, *m.* Nile River (in Egypt)

nīmīrum without doubt, certainly

nimis too, excessively

nimium too much, excessively

niteō, -ēre, nīsus sum to shine

nītor, -ī, nīxus sum to rely

niveus, -a, -um snowy

nōbilis, -e noble

nōlō, nōlle, nōluī to be unwilling, not want; (*imper.*) don't

nōn not; no

nōndum not yet

nōs, nostrum (nostrī), nōbīs, nōs, nōbīs we, us

noster, nostra, nostrum our, ours

nota, notae, *f.* character

nōtus, -a, -um known, familiar

nōvī, nōvisse, nōtus (*perf.* forms with *pres.* force) to know

novissimus, -a, -um latest, last; extreme

novus, -a, -um new

nox, noctis, *f.* night

nūbēs, nūbis, *f.* cloud

nūbō, -ere, nūpsī, nūptūrus (with *dat.*) to marry

nūdō, -āre, -āvī, -ātus to make bare

nūgae, nūgārum, *f.pl.* trifles

nūllus, -a, -um no, none, not; no one

num certainly...not?

nūmen, nūminis, *n.* divine power; divinity

numerus, numerī, *m.* number; meter

numquam never

nunc now

nūntiō, -āre, -āvī, -ātus to announce, tell

nūntius, nūntī, *m.* messenger; message

nūper recently

Nȳsigena, -ae, *m.adj.* born on Mount Nysa (birthplace of Bacchus)

O

ō oh

obdūrō, -āre, -āvī, -ātūrus to be persistent

oblectō, -āre, -āvī, -ātus to delight

oblitterō, -āre, -āvī, -ātus to cause to be forgotten

oblīvīscor, -ī, oblītus sum to forget

obscūrō, -āre, -āvī, -ātus to darken

obstinātus, -a, -um resolved, stubborn

obterō, -ere, obtrīvī, obtrītus to crush

obvius, -a, -um in the way; (with *dat.*) to meet

occidō, -ere, occidī, occāsūrus to fall, set

ocellus, ocellī, *m.* little eye; jewel, darling

octō eight

oculus, oculī, *m.* eye

ōdī, ōdisse, ōsus (*perf.* forms with *pres.* force) to hate

odium, odī, *n.* hatred

odor, odōris, *m.* scent, perfume

offerō, offerre, obtulī, oblātus to provide; to cause

officium, officī, *n.* duty

offīrmō, -āre, -āvī, -ātūrus to persist, persevere

olfaciō, -ere, olfēcī, olfactus to smell

ōlim once

omnipotēns, omnipotentis (*gen.*) all-powerful

omnis, -e all, every

onus, oneris, *n.* burden, load

opera, operae, *f.* effort

oportet, -ēre, oportuit to be necessary, be proper

opprimō, -ere, oppressī, oppressus to overwhelm

ops, opis, *f.* help, aid

optō, -āre, -āvī, -ātus to desire; to choose

opus, operis, *n.* need

ōrāc(u)lum, ōrāc(u)lī, *n.* oracle

ōrātiō, ōrātiōnis, *f.* speech

Orcus, Orcī, *m.* (god of the underworld); (the underworld)

orīgō, orīginis, *f.* beginning, source

ōrō, -āre, -āvī, -ātus to beg

Ortalus, Ortalī, *m.* (Quintus Hortensius (H)ortalus, orator, poet, and historian)

ōs, ōris, *n.* mouth; lip; face

ostendō, -ere, ostendī, ostentus to show

ostentō, -āre, -āvī, -ātus to indicate

ōtiōsus, -a, -um at leisure, idle

ōtium, ōtī, *n.* free time, leisure

P

paene īnsula, paene īnsulae, *f.* peninsula

paenitet, -ēre, -uit to regret: (*acc.*) regret (*gen.*)

palimpseston, -ī, *n.* palimpsest (papyrus recycled by erasure)

pallidulus, -a, -um pale

palmula, palmulae, *f.* oar

papilla, papillae, *f.* breast

papȳrus, papȳrī, *m.* papyrus, paper

pār, paris (*gen.*) equal, comparable

parātus, -a, -um ready, prepared

parcō, -ere, pepercī, parsūrus (with *infin.*) to refrain from

parēns, parentis, *m.f.* parent

parō, -āre, -āvī, -ātus to buy; to obtain

pars, partis, *f.* part

Parthī, Parthōrum, *m.pl.* Parthians

parvus, -a, -um little

passer, passeris, *m.* sparrow

passim here and there

pateō, -ēre, -uī to be open

pater, patris, *m.* father

paternus, -a, -um father's

patior, -ī, passus sum to allow

patrius, -a, -um father's

patrōna, patrōnae, *f.* patron

patrōnus, patrōnī, *m.* patron, advocate

paucī, paucae, pauca few

paulum for a little while

peccātum, peccātī, *n.* error, mistake, offense

pectus, pectoris, *n.* chest; heart

pelagus, pelagī, *n.* sea

pellō, -ere, pepulī, pulsus to drive; to strike

pendeō, -ēre, pependī to hang

penetrō, -āre, -āvī, -ātus to enter

per (with *acc.*) through, along

perditus, -a, -um desperate

perdō, -ere, perdidī, perditus to ruin, destroy; to lose

perdūcō, -ere, perdūxī, perductus to lead, conduct

peregrīnus, -a, -um foreign

perennis, -e through the years, enduring

pereō, perīre, periī, peritūrus to perish, die; to be desperately in love

perferō, perferre, pertulī, perlātus to carry on, endure

perfidus, -a, -um faithless, treacherous; deceitful

perhibeō, -ēre, -uī, -itus to say

periūrium, periūrī, *n.* false oath, perjury

perlūcidulus, -a, -um translucent

permulceō, -ēre, permulsī, permulsus to caress

perniciēs, perniciēī, *f.* ruin, destruction, disaster

pernumerō, -āre, -āvī, -ātus to count

perpetior, -ī, perpessus sum to allow, permit

perpetuus, -a, -um continuing, permanent

perscrībō, -ere, perscrīpsī, perscrīptus to write out fully

perspiciō, -ere, perspexī, perspectus to recognize

perūrō, -ere, perūssī, perūstus to burn up

perveniō, -īre, pervēnī, perventūrus to come, arrive

pervigilō, -āre, -āvī, -ātūrus to stay awake

pervincō, -ere, pervīcī, pervictus to defeat, overcome

pēs, pedis, *m.* foot; leg (of a bed); rope at lower part of a sail

pestilentia, pestilentiae, *f.* plague, pestilence

pestis, pestis, *f.* disease, plague; destruction

petītor, petītōris, *m.* candidate

petō, -ere, petīvī, petītus to seek

phasēlus, phasēlī, *m.* light ship

Phrygius, -a, -um Phrygian

pietās, pietātis, *f.* duty, devotion

pignus, pignoris, *n.* wager, stake

pilus, pilī, *m.* a hair; a bit

pīnus, pīnī, *f.* pine tree

pīpiō, -āre to chirp

Pīraeus, Pīraeī, *m.* (port of Athens)

pius, -a, -um dutiful, devoted

placeō, -ēre, -uī, -itūrus (with *dat.*) to please

plēnus, -a, -um full

plumbum, plumbī, *n.* lead (used for drawing lines)

plūrimum very (much)

plūs, plūris (*gen.*) more

poēma, poēmatis, *n.* poem

poena, poenae, *f.* penalty

poēta, poētae, *m.* poet

Polliō, Polliōnis, *m.* (Gaius Asinius Pollio, brother of the napkin thief)

pōnō, -ere, posuī, pos(i)tus to provide

Ponticus, -a, -um Pontic, of the Black Sea, on the Black Sea

pontus, pontī, *m.* sea

porrō forward, further

portō, -āre, -āvī, -ātus to carry

portus, portūs, *m.* port, harbor

possum, posse, potuī to be able

post (*adv.*) later, afterwards; (*prep.* with *acc.*) after

posthāc hereafter

postillā afterwards

postmodo later

postquam after

postrēmus, -a, -um final

potis (pote) able, possible

potius rather

prae (with *abl.*) before

praeceps, praecipitis (*gen.*) headlong

praeceptum, praeceptī, *n.* rule, precept

praecingō, -ere, praecīnxī, praecīnctus to encircle

praeda, praedae, *f.* prey

praegestiō, -īre to be very eager

praemium, praemī, *n.* reward

praeoptō, -āre, -āvī, -ātus to prefer

praeportō, -āre to carry in front

praeruptus, -a, -um steep

praesertim especially, particularly

praestō available, at hand

praetereā besides

praetereō, -īre, praeteriī, praeteritus to go past; to surpass

praetor, praetōris, *m.* governor

praetrepidō, -āre to tremble in anticipation

prātum, prātī, *n.* meadow

pretium, pretī, *n.* price, cost

prex, precis, *f.* prayer

prīmum first; (taken with *cum*) as soon as; (taken with *quam*) as soon as possible

prīmus, -a, -um first; first part of, tip of

prior, prius earlier, previous

prīscus, -a, -um ancient; old-fashioned

prius before, previously, earlier

prō (with *abl.*) for, on behalf of; in return for

probē well

procella, procellae, *f.* storm

prōcreō, -āre, -āvī, -ātus to create, produce

procul far away, far off

prōcurrō, -ere, prōcucurrī, prōcursūrus to run forward

prōdō, -ere, prōdidī, prōditus to betray

prōferō, prōferre, prōtulī, prōlātus to bring forth

proficīscor, -ī, profectus sum to set out, proceed

prōfundō, -ere, prōfūdī, prōfūsus to pour forth

prōiciō, -ere, prōiēcī, prōiectus to give up; to sacrifice

prōmissum, prōmissī, *n.* promise

prōmittō, -ere, prōmīsī, prōmissus to promise

prōnus, -a, -um leaning forward; prone; sloping

prope nearly, almost

prōpōnō, -ere, prōposuī, prōpositus to propose

Propontis, Propontidis, *f.* (*acc.:* **Propontida**) Propontis, Sea of Marmora

prōsiliō, -īre, prōsiluī to leap forth

prōspectō, -āre, -āvī, -ātus to gaze out at

prōspectus, prōspectūs, *m.* view

prōsperus, -a, -um favorable

prōspiciō, -ere, prōspexī, prōspectus to watch

prōsternō, -ere, prōstrāvī, prōstrātus to overthrow

prōsum, prōdesse, prōfuī to be of use, be beneficial

prōtendō, -ere, —, prōtentus to stretch out, extend

prōvincia, prōvinciae, *f.* province

-pte (emphatic particle)

pudīcus, -a, -um modest, chaste

puella, puellae, *f.* girl; girlfriend

puer, puerī, *m.* boy

pulcerrimus, -a, -um very beautiful

pulvis, pulveris, *m.* dust

pūmex, pūmicis, *f.* pumice

puppis, puppis, *f.* ship

pūriter in a pure manner

purpureus, -a, -um purple

pūrus, -a, -um plain white

putō, -āre, -āvī, -ātus to think

Q

quā where

quaerō, -ere, quaesīvī, quaesītus to ask, ask for, seek

quaesō please

quālis, -e what (sort of); such as, like, as

quāliscumque, quālecumque of whatever quality, such as it is

quālubet no matter how

quam how; than; (with *tam*) as; (taken with *ante* or *prius*) before

quamvīs ever so; although

quandō ever

quandoquidem since

quantō (with *tantō*) as

quantum whatever amount; as much as; (with *tantus*) as

quantus, -a, -um how much; what great; (with *tantus*) as

quāre for what reason, why; therefore

quasi as if

quassō, -āre, -āvī, -ātus to shake repeatedly

quatiō, -ere, —, quassus to shake

-que and, both

queō, quīre, quīvī to be able

quercus, quercūs, *f.* oak tree

querella, querellae, *f.* lament, complaint

questus, questūs, *m.* complaint

quī, quae, quod who, which, that; any; what

quī (*adv.*) how

quīcumque, quaecumque, quodcumque whoever, whatever

quid (*adv.*) why

quīdam, quaedam, quoddam certain

quiēs, quiētis, *f.* rest

quīn why not; that

quīnam, quaenam, quodnam (just) which, (just) what

Quīntia, Quīntiae, *f.* (name of a beautiful woman)

Quīntilia, Quīntiliae, *f.* (Calvus' wife or mistress)

quis, quid who, what; anyone, anything

quisquam, quicquam anyone, anything

quisque, quaeque, quidque each one

quisquis, quidquid whoever, whatever

quīvīs, quaevīs, quidvīs any

quīvīs cumque, quaevīs cumque, quodvīs cumque every conceivable

quō where, to what place

quod because; the fact that; (with *sī*) but

quondam once, formerly

quoniam since

quoque also

quot how many, as many as

R

rādīcitus by the roots

rāmus, rāmī, *m.* branch

rapāx, rapācis (*gen.*) grasping, rapacious

rapidus, -a, -um swift, rapid

rārus, -a, -um uncommon, rare

ratiō, ratiōnis, *f.* reason; method

ratis, ratis, *f.* boat, ship

Rāvidus, Rāvidī, *m.* (acquaintance of Catullus)

recipiō, -ere, recēpī, receptus to take up again; to receive

recondō, -ere, recondidī, reconditus to conceal, seclude

recordor, -ārī, -ātus sum to remember

rēctor, rēctōris, *m.* ruler

rēctus, -a, -um straight-backed; stately

recūrō, -āre, -āvī, -ātus to restore

reddō, -ere, reddidī, redditus to give back, return; to deliver

redeō, redīre, rediī, reditūrus to go back, return

redimiō, -īre, —, -ītus to encircle, crown

redūcō, -ere, redūxī, reductus to lead back, bring back

redux, reducis (*gen.*) returned

referō, referre, rettulī, relātus to bring back; to record

reficiō, -ere, refēcī, refectus to renew

reflectō, -ere, reflexī, reflexus to turn back; to bend back

rēgius, -a, -um royal, splendid

regō, -ere, rēxī, rēctus to rule; to guide

religō, -āre, -āvī, -ātus to untie

relinquō, -ere, relīquī, relictus to leave, abandon

remittō, -ere, remīsī, remissus to send back, return

remūneror, -ārī, -ātus sum to pay back

rēmus, rēmī, *m.* oar

renovō, -āre, -āvī, -ātus to renew, restore

repente suddenly

reperiō, -īre, repperī, repertus to find, discover

repōnō, -ere, reposuī, repositus to put back, put down

reportō, -āre, -āvī, -ātus to bring back, return

reposcō, -ere to demand

requiēscō, -ere, requiēvī to rest; to find relief

requīrō, -ere, requīsīvī, requīsītus to ask, seek; to miss

rēs, reī, *f.* thing, matter; case, respect

resonō, -āre, -āvī to echo, resound

respectō, -āre, -āvī, -ātus to wait for, expect

respergō, -ere, respersī, respersus to sprinkle

respondeō, -ēre, respondī, respōnsus to answer, reply

restituō, -ere, restituī, restitūtus to restore; to revive

retineō, -ēre, -uī, retentus to hold back, keep

retrahō, -ere, retrāxī, retractus to withdraw, remove

revocō, -āre, -āvī, -ātus to call back

rēx, rēgis, *m.* king

Rhēnus, Rhēnī, *m.* Rhine river

Rhodus, Rhodī, *f.* Rhodes (island off the coast of Asia Minor)

Rhoetēus, -a, -um of Rhoeteum (promontory and city near Troy)

rīdeō, -ēre, rīsī, rīsus to laugh, laugh at

rixa, rixae, *f.* quarrel

rōbur, rōboris, *f.* trunk (of a tree)

rogō, -āre, -āvī, -ātus to ask, ask for

Rōma, Rōmae, *f.* Rome

Rōmulus, Rōmulī, *m.* (legendary founder of Rome)

rubeō, -ēre to be red, become red

ruber, rubra, rubrum red

rubor, rubōris, *m.* blush

rudēns, rudentis, *m.* rope

Rūfus, Rūfī, *m.* (perhaps Marcus Caelius Rufus, Clodia's lover)

rumor, rumōris, *m.* rumor, gossip

rumpō, -ere, rūpī, ruptus to break, burst

rūpēs, rūpis, *f.* rock, cliff

rūrsus on the other hand

rūs, rūris, *n.* country

S

Sabīnus, -a, -um Sabine

sacculus, sacculī, *m.* purse

sacer, sacra, sacrum sacred; accursed

saec(u)lum, saec(u)lī, *n.* generation

saepe often

Saetabus, -a, -um of Saetabis (a town in Spain)

saevus, -a, -um savage

Sagae, Sagārum, *m.pl.* (a Scythian people)

sagittifer, sagittifera, sagittiferum arrow-
bearing

sāl, salis, *m.* salt; wit; sea

salsus, -a, -um witty, funny

salūs, salūtis, *f.* health; salvation

salvē hello, hail

sānctus, -a, -um holy, sacred

sānē really, truly

sanguis, sanguinis, *m.* blood

sapiō, -ere, sapīvī to have taste, be wise

Sapphicus, -a, -um Sapphic, of Sappho

satiō, -āre, -āvī, -ātus to satisfy

satis enough

Sāturnālia, Sāturnālium, *n.pl.* (festival of
Saturn)

saturō, -āre, -āvī, -ātus to satisfy

Satyrus, Satyrī, *m.* Satyr (part man, part goat)

saucius, -a, -um wounded

saxeus, -a, -um stony

scelestus, -a, -um wretched, wicked

scīlicet of course, surely

sciō, -īre, -īvī, -ītus to know

scītus, -a, -um smart, clever

scopulus, scopulī, *m.* cliff

scortillum, scortillī, *n.* little prostitute

scrībō, -ere, scrīpsī, scrīptus to write

scrīnium, scrīnī, *n.* cylindrical case (for holding
scrolls)

scrīptor, scrīptōris, *m.* writer

scrīptum, scrīptī, *n.* writing

scurra, scurrae, *m.* witty person

Scylla, Scyllae, *f.* (half-human sea monster)

sēcēdō, -ere, sēcessī, sēcessūrus to withdraw

sector, -ārī, -ātus sum to follow, pursue, chase

secundus, -a, -um favorable; second

sed but

sedeō, -ēre, sēdī, sessūrus to sit

sēdēs, sēdis, *f.* home

semel a single time, once and for all

sēmimortuus, -a, -um half dead

semper always

senecta, senectae, *f.* old age

seneō, -ēre to be old

senex, senis, *m.* old man

sēnsus, sēnsūs, *m.* sense

sentiō, -īre, sēnsī, sēnsus to feel, perceive; to
understand

sepeliō, -īre, sepelīvī, sepultus to bury

septemgeminus, -a, -um seven-mouthed

Septimillus, Septimillī, *m.* dear Septimius

Septimius, Septimī, *m.* (lover of Acme)

sepulcrum, sepulcrī, *n.* tomb

sequor, -ī, secūtus sum to follow

Serāpis, Serāpis, *m.* Serapis (Egyptian god of
healing)

sermō, sermōnis, *m.* talk, conversation

serō, -ere, sēvī, satus to sow, plant

serva, servae, *f.* slave

serviō, -īre, -īvī, -ītūrus (with *dat.*) to serve

Sestiānus, -a, -um Sestian, of Sestius

Sestius, Sestī, *m.* (Publius Sestius, defended by
Cicero)

seu or, whether; or if

sevērus, -a, -um strict, severe, serious

sēvocō, -āre, -āvī, -ātus to call away

sī if

sībilus, sībilī, *m.* whistling, hissing

sīc in this way, so, thus

siccus, -a, -um dry

sīcine is this the way?

sīcut just as

sīdus, sīderis, *n.* star

signum, signī, *n.* sign, signal

Sīlēnus, Sīlēnī, *m.* (attendant of Bacchus)

silēscō, -ere to become silent

silva, silvae, *f.* forest

simul at the same time; together; as soon as; (with *ac*) as soon

sincērē sincerely

sine (with *abl.*) without

singulī, singulae, singula individual

singultus, singultūs, *m.* sob

sinister, sinistra, sinistrum left

sinistra, sinistrae, *f.* left, left side

sinō, -ere, sīvī, sītus to allow

sinus, sinūs, *m.* breast; lap; bay

sīquī, sīqua, sīquod if any

Sirmiō, Sirmiōnis, *f.* (promontory on Lake Benacus)

sistō, -ere, stitī, stātus to establish; to present

sīve or, whether

sodālis, sodālis, *m.* companion, friend

sōl, sōlis, *m.* sun

sōlāciolum, sōlāciolī, *n.* a little comfort

soleō, -ēre, solitus sum to be accustomed

sōlus, -a, -um alone, only; lonely

solvō, -ere, soluī, solūtus to loosen; to release; to fulfill

somnus, somnī, *m.* sleep

sonitus, sonitūs, *m.* sound

sordidus, -a, -um vile, crude

sōspes, sōspitis (*gen.*) safe, unhurt

spectō, -āre, -āvī, -ātus to watch, look at

spērō, -āre, -āvī, -ātus to hope, hope for

spēs, speī, *f.* hope

spīnōsus, -a, -um spiny

spōnsus, spōnsī, *m.* bridegroom

spūmō, -āre, -āvī, -ātus to foam

spūmōsus, -a, -um foamy

stāgnum, stāgnī, *n.* standing water, pool

statua, statuae, *f.* statue

sternuō, -ere, sternuī to sneeze

stīpendium, stīpendī, *n.* tribute

stō, stāre, stetī, stātūrus to stand

strophium, strophī, *n.* breastband

studiōsus, -a, -um eager

studium, studī, *n.* enthusiasm

suāvior, -ārī, -ātus sum to kiss

suāvis, -e pleasant

sub (with *acc.* or *abl.*) under

subitō suddenly

sublevō, -āre, -āvī, -ātus to encourage

subrēpō, -ere, subrēpsī, subrēptūrus to creep up

subter (with *abl.*) under

subtīlis, -e delicate

suburbānus, -a, -um suburban

succipiō, -ere, succēpī, succeptus to undertake

sūdārium, sūdārī, *n.* napkin

sūdō, -āre, -āvī, -ātus to sweat

Suffēnus, Suffēnī, *m.* (bad Roman poet ridiculed by Catullus)

—, suī, sibi, sē (sēsē), sē (sēsē) himself, herself, itself, themselves

Sulla, Sullae, *m.* (Roman schoolmaster)

sum, esse, fuī, futūrus to be; (with *male* or *malignē*) to go

summus, -a, -um top of

sūmō, -ere, sūmpsī, sūmptus to take up, undertake

sūmptuōsus, -a, -um expensive, lavish

super more

superbus, -a, -um proud

superō, -āre, -āvī, -ātus to surpass

supplex, supplicis (*gen.*) humble, suppliant

supplicium, supplicī, *n.* punishment

suppōnō, -ere, supposuī, suppositus to place (*acc.*) under (*dat.*), place (*acc.*) next to (*dat.*)

suprēmus, -a, -um final

sūra, sūrae, *f.* calf (of the leg)

surripiō, -ere, surripuī, surreptus to steal

suspendō, -ere, suspendī, suspēnsus to hang

suspicor, -ārī, -ātus sum to suspect

suspīrō, -āre, -āvī, -ātus to sigh

sustollō, -ere to raise

suus, -a, -um his, her, its, their (own)

Syria, Syriae, *f.* (country in Asia Minor)

Syrtis, Syrtis, *f.* (sand bank off the coast of North Africa)

T

tabella, tabellae, *f.* tablet

taberna, tabernae, *f.* inn

taceō, -ēre, -uī, -itus to be silent, be quiet

tacitus, -a, -um silent, quiet; secret

taeter, taetra, taetrum foul, vile, horrible

talentum, talentī, *n.* a talent (a Greek unit of weight)

tālis, -e such

tam so; (with *quam*) as

tamen however, still, nevertheless

tangō, -ere, tetigī, tāctus to touch; to reach

tantō (with *quantō*) as great, as much

tantum such a great quantity; so; only; (with *quantum*) as much

tantus, -a, -um such great, so great; (with *quantus*) as great, as much

tardipēs, tardipedis (*gen.*) slow-footed

taurus, taurī, *m.* bull

Taurus, Taurī, *m.* Taurus (mountain range in south of Asia Minor)

tēctum, tēctī, *n.* house, building

tegmen, tegminis, *n.* covering

tegō, -ere, tēxī, tēctus to cover

tellūs, tellūris, *f.* earth

tēlum, tēlī, *n.* spear, missile

tempestās, tempestātis, *f.* time

templum, templī, *n.* temple

temptō, -āre, -āvī, -ātus to try

tempus, temporis, *n.* time; need

tēn = tēne

tenēbrae, tenēbrārum, *f.pl.* darkness

tenēbricōsus, -a, -um dark

teneō, -ēre, -uī, tentus to hold

tener, tenera, tenerum tender, delicate

tenuis, -e thin

tepefactō, -āre to make warm, warm

tepor, tepōris, *m.* warmth

teres, teretis (*gen.*) smooth, rounded

tergum, tergī, *n.* back

terra, terrae, *f.* land, earth

Thēseus, Thēseī, *m.* (*acc.*: **Thēsea**; *voc.*: **Thēseu**) (son of Aegeus)

thiasus, thiasī, *m.* band, chorus

Thrācius, -a, -um Thracian

Thūnia, Thūniae, *f.* Thynia (country of the Thynii); Bithynia

Tīburs, Tīburtis (*gen.*) of Tibur, Tiburtine

timor, timōris, *m.* fear

tintinō, -āre to ring

tollō, -ere, sustulī, sublātus to lift up, raise; to take away

torpeō, -ēre, -uī to be numb, be paralyzed

torpor, torpōris, *m.* numbness, paralysis

torreō, -ēre, -uī, tostus to parch, scorch

tot so many

tōtus, -a, -um all, whole, entire

trabs, trabis, *f.* boat, ship

trādō, -ere, trādidī, trāditus to hand over, deliver; to entrust

trāns (with *acc.*) across

trecentī, trecentae, trecenta three hundred

tremulus, -a, -um trembling, rippling

trēs, tria three

tribuō, -ere, tribuī, tribūtus to grant, bestow

trīstis, -e sad

Trōius, -a, -um Trojan

truculentus, -a, -um savage, ferocious

trux, trucis (*gen.*) wild, harsh, fierce

tū, tuī, tibi, tē (tētē), tē (tētē) you (*s.*)

tueor, -ērī, -itus sum to see

Tullius, Tullī, *m.* (Marcus Tullius Cicero, orator and politician)

tum then, at that moment; (with *cum*) but also

tumulō, -āre, -āvī, -ātus to bury

tunc then, at that time

tundō, -ere, tutudī, tūnsus to beat repeatedly, pound

turbō, turbinis, *m.* tornado, whirlwind

turgidulus, -a, -um poor swollen

turpis, -e disgraceful

tussis, tussis, *f.* cough

tūte (emphatic form of *tū*) you (*s.*)

tūtum, tūtī, *n.* safe place, safety

tūtus, -a, -um safe

tuus, -a, -um your, yours (*s.*)

U

ūber, ūberis (*gen.*) fertile, rich

ubi where

ūdus, -a, -um wet

ulcīscor, -ī, ultus sum to take revenge on, punish

ūllus, -a, -um any

ultimus, -a, -um earliest; farthest; edge of

ultrō willingly

umbilīcus, umbilīcī, *m.* knob (ornamental end of a papyrus roll cylinder)

umbra, umbrae, *f.* shadow, shade

umquam ever

ūnā together

ūnanimus, -a, -um like-minded

ūnctus, -a, -um well-oiled, slick

unda, undae, *f.* wave; water

unde from where; from which

undique on all sides

unguentum, unguentī, *n.* perfume

ūnicus, -a, -um one and only

ūnus, -a, -um one; alone, only

urbānus, -a, -um urbane, sophisticated

urbs, urbis, *f.* city

Ūriī, Ūriōrum, *m.pl.* (Italian town associated with the cult of Venus)

ūrō, -ere, ussī, ūstus to burn

urtīca, urtīcae, *f.* nettle, stinging-nettle

usque all the way; continuously

ūstulō, -āre, -āvī, -ātus to burn, scorch

ut (utī) as, when; like; where; how; so that, that

uterque, utraque, utrumque each

utinam if only

ūtor, -ī, ūsus sum (with *abl.*) to use

utpote naturally since

utrum whether

V

vacuus, -a, -um empty

vadum, vadī, *n.* water

vae alas; (with *acc.*) woe to, alas for

vagor, -ārī, -ātus sum to wander, roam

vagus, -a, -um wandering

valdē very

valeō, -ēre, -uī, -itūrus to be strong, be well; to prevail; (*imper.*) goodbye

vallēs, vallis, *f.* valley

vānēscō, -ere to vanish

vānus, -a, -um empty

variē in different ways

variō, -āre, -āvī, -ātus to adorn

varius, -a, -um different, various

Vārus, Vārī, *m.* (friend of Catullus)

vastus, -a, -um huge; monstrous

Vatīniānus, -a, -um of Vatinius, against Vatinius

-ve or

vēcors, vēcordis (*gen.*) senseless, demented

vehō, -ere, vexī, vectus to carry

vel even

vēlō, -āre, -āvī, -ātus to cover

vēlum, vēlī, *n.* sail

velut just as, as

vēmēns, vēmentis (*gen.*) violent, powerful

venēnum, venēnī, *n.* poison

veniō, -īre, vēnī, ventūrus to come

vēnor, -ārī, -ātus sum to hunt

venter, ventris, *m.* belly, stomach

ventitō, -āre, -āvī, -ātūrus to come often

ventōsus, -a, -um windy

ventus, ventī, *m.* wind

Venus, Veneris, *f.* (goddess of love); love, charm

venustās, venustātis, *f.* charm, grace, attraction

venustus, -a, -um charming, attractive

vēr, vēris, *n.* spring

Vērāniolus, Vērāniolī, *m.* dear Veranius

Vērānius, Vērānī, *m.* (friend of Catullus)

verbum, verbī, *n.* word

vernus, -a, -um spring-, vernal

vērō truly

Vērōna, Vērōnae, *f.* (birthplace of Catullus)

versiculus, versiculī, *n.* light verse, short verse

versō, -āre, -āvī, -ātus to turn

versor, -ārī, -ātus sum to toss and turn

versus, versūs, *m.* verse

vertex, verticis, *f.* summit; head

vērum but

vērus, -a, -um true

vēsānus, -a, -um insane, crazy

vester, vestra, vestrum your, yours (*pl.*)

vestīgium, vestīgī, *n.* sole (bottom of the foot); footprint, track

vestis, vestis, *f.* garment, clothing; coverlet, bedspread

vetus, veteris (*gen.*) old

vexō, -āre, -āvī, -ātus to disturb, trouble

via, viae, *f.* way, path, route

vibrō, -āre, -āvī, -ātus to hurl

—, vicis, *f.* condition, situation

videō, -ēre, vīdī, vīsus to see; (*pass.*) to be seen, seem

vigeō, -ēre, -uī to thrive

vigēscō, -ere, viguī to become lively

vīlis, -e cheap, worthless

vīlla, vīllae, *f.* country house

vinciō, -īre, vīnxī, vīnctus to bind

vindex, vindicis (*gen.*) avenging

vīnum, vīnī, *n.* wine

violō, -āre, -āvī, -ātus to violate, dishonor

vir, virī, *m.* man

virgō, virginis, *f.* maiden

virtūs, virtūtis, *f.* courage; virtue

vīsō, -ere, vīsī to go to see, visit; to see

vīta, vītae, *f.* life

vīvō, -ere, vīxī, vīctūrus to live

vix hardly, scarcely

vocō, -āre, -āvī, -ātus to call, summon, invite

volitō, -āre, -āvī, -ātus to fly about

volō, -āre, -āvī, -ātūrus to fly; to speed

volō, velle, voluī to wish, want; to like; (taken with *bene*) to like

voluntās, voluntātis, *f.* will, wish

voluptās, voluptātis, *f.* pleasure

Volusius, Volusī, *m.* (bad poet, author of the *Annālēs*)

volvō, -ere, volvī, volūtus to turn

vorō, -āre, -āvī, -ātus to devour, eat up

vōs, vestrum, vōbīs, vōs, vōbīs you (*pl.*)

vōtum, vōtī, *n.* vow, prayer; votive offering

voveō, -ēre, vōvī, vōtus to promise, vow

vōx, vōcis, *f.* voice; word

vulgus, vulgī, *n.* common people, general public

vultus, vultūs, *m.* face

Z

Zephyrus, Zephyrī, *m.* Zephyr (West Wind)

1. REGULAR VERBS

In Latin the verb is especially important. It causes the subject either to act or to be acted upon. It expresses mood, voice, tense, person, and number. It includes four participles, the gerund, and the supine.

The present, imperfect, and the future indicative tenses, active and passive, are formed from the *present stem,* obtained by removing the -re from the present infinitive. The three perfect indicative active tenses are formed from the *perfect stem,* obtained by removing the -ī from the third principal part. The three perfect indicative passive tenses are formed from the fourth principal part, the entire *perfect passive participle.*

First Conjugation

PRINCIPAL PARTS OF LAUDŌ
laudō, Pres. Ind., Act., lst Sing.,   *I praise*
laudāre, Pres. Inf. Act.,   *to praise*
laudāvī, Perf. Ind. Act., 1st Sing.,   *I have praised, I praised*
laudātus, Perf. Pass. Part.,   *having been praised*

PARTICIPLES
Present Active: laudāns   *praising*
Perfect Passive: laudātus, -a, -um   *having been praised*
Future Active: laudātūrus, -a, -um   *being about to praise*
Gerundive: laudandus, -a, -um   *worthy to be praised*

INDICATIVE ACTIVE

Present		*Perfect*	
laudō	*I praise*	laudāvī	*I have praised*
laudās	*you...*	laudāvistī	*you have...*
laudat	*he praises*	laudāvit	*he has...*
laudāmus	*we praise*	laudāvimus	*we have...*
laudātis	*you...*	laudāvistis	*you have...*
laudant	*they...*	laudāvērunt	*they have...*
Imperfect		*Pluperfect*	
laudābam	*I was praising*	laudāveram	*I had praised*
laudābās	*you were...*	laudāverās	*you had...*
laudābat	*he was...*	laudāverat	*he had...*
laudābāmus	*we were...*	laudāverāmus	*we had...*
laudābātis	*you were...*	laudāverātis	*you had...*
laudābant	*they were...*	laudāverant	*they had...*
Future		*Future Perfect*	
laudābō	*I shall praise*	laudāverō	*I shall have praised*
laudābis	*you will...*	laudāveris	*you will have...*
laudābit	*he will...*	laudāverit	*he will have...*
laudābimus	*we will...*	laudāverimus	*we will have...*
laudābitis	*you will...*	laudāveritis	*you will have...*
laudābunt	*they will...*	laudāverint	*they will have...*

INDICATIVE PASSIVE

Present		*Future*		*Pluperfect*	
laudor	*I am (being) praised*	laudābor	*I shall be praised*	laudātus, -a, -um **eram**	*I had been praised*
laudāris	*you are...*	laudāberis	*you will be...*	laudātus, -a, -um **erās**	*you had been...*
laudātur	*he is...*	laudābitur	*he will be...*	laudātus, -a, -um **erat**	*he had been...*
laudāmur	*we are...*	laudābimur	*we shall be...*	laudātī, -ae, -a **erāmus**	*we had been...*
laudāminī	*you are...*	laudābiminī	*you will be...*	laudātī, -ae, -a **erātis**	*you had been...*
laudantur	*they are...*	laudābuntur	*they will be...*	laudātī, -ae, -a **erant**	*they had been...*
Imperfect		*Perfect*		*Future Perfect*	
laudābar	*I was being praised*	laudātus, -a, -um **sum**	*I have been praised*	laudātus, -a, -um **erō**	*I shall have been praised*
laudābāris	*you were...*	laudātus, -a, -um **es**	*you have been...*	laudātus, -a, -um **eris**	*you will have been...*
laudābātur	*he was...*	laudātus, -a, -um **est**	*he has been...*	laudātus, -a, -um **erit**	*he will have been...*
laudābāmur	*we were...*	laudātī, -ae, -a **sumus**	*we have been...*	laudātī, -ae, -a **erimus**	*we shall have been...*
laudābāminī	*you were...*	laudātī, -ae, -a **estis**	*you have been...*	laudātī, -ae, -a **eritis**	*you will have been...*
laudābantur	*they were...*	laudātī, -ae, -a **sunt**	*they have been...*	laudātī, -ae, -a **erunt**	*they will have been...*

INFINITIVES
ACTIVE
Present: laudāre   *to praise*
Perfect: laudāvisse   *to have praised*
Future: laudātūrus esse   *to be about to praise*
PASSIVE
Present: laudārī   *to be praised*
Perfect: laudātus esse   *to have been praised*
Future: laudātum īrī (rare)   *to be about to be praised*

GERUND
Nominative: laudāre   *praising*
Genitive: laudandī   *of praising*
Dative: laudandō   *for praising*
Accusative: laudandum   *praising*
Ablative: laudandō   *by praising*

SUBJUNCTIVE ACTIVE[1]

Present	*Perfect*
laudem	laudāverim
laudēs	laudāverīs
laudet	laudāverit
laudēmus	laudāverīmus
laudētis	laudāverītus
laudent	laudāverint
Imperfect	*Pluperfect*
laudārem	laudāvissem
laudārēs	laudāvissēs
laudāret	laudāvisset
laudārēmus	laudāvissēmus
laudārētis	laudāvissētis
laudārent	laudāvissent

SUBJUNCTIVE PASSIVE

Present	*Perfect*	
lauder	laudātus, -a, -um	**sim**
laudēris	laudātus, -a, -um	**sīs**
laudētur	laudātus, -a, -um	**sit**
laudēmur	laudātī, -ae, -a	**sīmus**
laudēminī	laudātī, -ae, -a	**sītis**
laudentur	laudātī, -ae, -a	**sint**
Imperfect	*Pluperfect*	
laudārer	laudātus, -a, -um	**essem**
laudārēris	laudātus, -a, -um	**essēs**
laudārētur	laudātus, -a, -um	**esset**
laudārēmur	laudātī, -ae, -a	**essēmus**
laudārēminī	laudātī, -ae, -a	**essētis**
laudārentur	laudātī, -ae, -a	**essent**

[1]No meanings are given for the subjunctive because of the great variety of its uses. Each use calls for its own, special translation.

SUPINE
laudātum   *to praise*
laudātū   *to praise*

IMPERATIVE ACTIVE
PRESENT
Sing.: laudā   *praise*
Plur.: laudāte   *praise*

IMPERATIVE PASSIVE
PRESENT
Sing.: laudāre   *be praised*
Plur.: laudāminī   *be praised*

Second Conjugation

PRINCIPAL PARTS OF MONEŌ
moneō   *I warn*   **monuī**   *I have warned*
monēre   *to warn*   **monitus**   *warned*

SUPINE
monitum
monitū

PARTICIPLES
Present Act.: monēns   *warning*
Perfect Pass.: monitus, -a, -um
Future Act.: monitūrus, -a, -um
Gerundive: monendus, -a, -um

GERUND
Nom.: monēre
Gen.: monendī
Dat.: monendō
Acc.: monendum
Abl.: monendō

INFINITIVES
ACTIVE
Present: **monēre**
Perfect: **monuisse**
Future: **monitūrus esse**
PASSIVE
Present: mōnērī
Perfect: monitus esse
Future: monitum īrī

INDICATIVE ACTIVE

Present	*Perfect*
moneō	monuī
monēs	monuistī
monet	monuit
monēmus	monuimus
monētis	monuistis
monent	monuērunt
Imperfect	*Pluperfect*
monēbam	monueram
monēbās	monuerās
monēbat	monuerat
monēbāmus	monuerāmus
monēbātis	monuerātis
monēbant	monuerant
Future	*Future Perfect*
monēbō	monuerō
monēbis	monueris
monēbit	monuerit
monēbimus	monuerimus
monēbitis	monueritis
monēbunt	monuerint

INDICATIVE PASSIVE

Present	*Perfect*
moneor	monitus, -a, -um **sum**
monēris	monitus, -a, -um **es**
monētur	monitus, -a, -um **est**
monēmur	monitī, -ae, -a **sumus**
monēminī	monitī, -ae, -a **estis**
monentur	monitī, -ae, -a **sunt**
Imperfect	*Pluperfect*
monēbar	monitus, -a, -um **eram**
monēbāris	monitus, -a, -um **erās**
monēbātur	monitus, -a, -um **erat**
monēbāmur	monitī, -ae, -a **erāmus**
monēbāminī	monitī, -ae, -a **erātis**
monēbantur	monitī, -ae, -a **erant**
Future	*Future Perfect*
monēbor	monitus, -a, -um **erō**
monēberis	monitus, -a, -um **eris**
monēbitur	monitus, -a, -um **erit**
monēbimur	monitī, -ae, -a **erimus**
monēbiminī	monitī, -ae, -a **eritis**
monēbuntur	monitī, -ae, -a **erunt**

IMPERATIVE ACT.
PRESENT
Sing.: monē
Plur.: monēte

IMPERATIVE PASS.
PRESENT
Sing.: monēre
Plur.: monēminī

SUBJUNCTIVE ACT.

Present	*Perfect*
moneam	monuerim
moneās	monuerīs
moneat	monuerit
moneāmus	monuerīmus
moneātis	monuerītis
moneant	monuerint
Imperfect	*Pluperfect*
monērem	monuissem
monērēs	monuissēs
monēret	monuisset
monērēmus	monuissēmus
monērētis	monuissētis
monērent	monuissent

SUBJUNCTIVE PASS.

Present	*Perfect*
monear	monitus, -a, -um **sim**
moneāris	monitus, -a, -um **sīs**
moneātur	monitus, -a, -um **sit**
moneāmur	monitī, -ae, -a **sīmus**
moneāminī	monitī, -ae, -a **sītis**
moneantur	monitī, -ae, -a **sint**
Imperfect	*Pluperfect*
monērer	monitus, -a, -um **essem**
monērēris	monitus, -a, -um **essēs**
monērētur	monitus, -a, -um **esset**
monērēmur	monitī, -ae, -a **essēmus**
monērēminī	monitī, -ae, -a **essētis**
monērentur	monitī, -ae, -a **essent**

Third Conjugation

PRINCIPAL PARTS OF DŪCŌ

dūcō	*I lead*	**dūxī**	*I have led*
dūcere	*to lead*	**ductus**	*having been led*

The future active of the third conjugation is formed by adding -am, -ēs, -et, etc. to the present stem minus **-e**. To form the passive, -ar, -ēris, ētur, etc. are added to the present stem minus **-e**.

INDICATIVE ACTIVE

Present	Perfect
dūcō	dūxī
dūcis	dūxistī
dūcit	dūxit
dūcimus	dūximus
dūcitis	dūxistis
dūcunt	dūxērunt
Imperfect	*Pluperfect*
dūcēbam	dūxeram
dūcēbās	dūxerās
dūcēbat	dūxerat
dūcēbāmus	dūxerāmus
dūcēbātis	dūxerātis
dūcēbant	dūxerant
Future	*Future Perf.*
dūcam	dūxerō
dūcēs	dūxeris
dūcet	dūxerit
dūcēmus	dūxerimus
dūcētis	dūxeritis
dūcent	dūxerint

INDICATIVE PASSIVE

Present	Perfect
dūcor	ductus, -a, -um **sum**
dūceris	ductus, -a, -um **es**
dūcitur	ductus, -a, -um **est**
dūcimur	ductī, -ae, -a **sumus**
dūciminī	ductī, -ae, -a **estis**
dūcuntur	ductī, -ae, -a **sunt**
Imperfect	*Pluperfect*
dūcēbar	ductus, -a, -um **eram**
dūcēbāris	ductus, -a, -um **erās**
dūcēbātur	ductus, -a, -um **erat**
dūcēbāmur	ductī, -ae, -a **erāmus**
dūcēbāminī	ductī, -ae, -a **erātis**
dūcēbantur	ductī, -ae, -a **erant**
Future	*Future Perfect*
dūcar	ductus, -a, -um **erō**
dūcēris	ductus, -a, -um **eris**
dūcētur	ductus, -a, -um **erit**
dūcēmur	ductī, -ae, -a **erimus**
dūcēminī	ductī, -ae, -a **eritis**
dūcentur	ductī, -ae, -a **erunt**

SUBJUNCTIVE ACT.

Present	Perfect
dūcam	dūxerim
dūcās	dūxerīs
dūcat	dūxerit
dūcāmus	dūxerīmus
dūcātis	dūxerītis
dūcant	dūxerint
Imperfect	*Pluperfect*
dūcerem	dūxissem
dūcerēs	dūxissēs
dūceret	dūxisset
dūcerēmus	dūxissēmus
dūcerētis	dūxissētis
dūcerent	dūxissent

IMPERATIVE ACTIVE

Sing.: dūc[1]
Plur.: dūcite

[1]There are 4 verbs whose imperative omits the final "e" in the singular: dīc, dūc, fer, fac.

SUBJUNCTIVE PASSIVE

Present	Perfect
dūcar	ductus, -a, -um **sim**
dūcāris	ductus, -a, -um **sīs**
dūcātur	ductus, -a, -um **sit**
dūcāmur	ductī, -ae, -a **sīmus**
dūcāminī	ductī, -ae, -a **sītis**
dūcantur	ductī, -ae, -a **sint**
Imperfect	*Pluperfect*
dūcerer	ductus, -a, -um **essem**
dūcerēris	ductus, -a, -um **essēs**
dūcerētur	ductus, -a, -um **esset**
dūcerēmur	ductī, -ae, -a **essēmus**
dūcerēminī	ductī, -ae, -a **essētis**
dūcerentur	ductī, -ae, -a **essent**

IMPERATIVE PASSIVE

Sing.: dūcere
Plur.: dūciminī

PARTICIPLES

Present Active: dūcēns, dūcentis
Perf. Passive: ductus, -a, -um
Fut. Active: ductūrus, -a, -um
Gerundive: dūcendus, -a, -um

INFINITIVES

ACTIVE
Pres.: dūcere
Perf.: dūxisse
Fut.: ductūrus esse
PASSIVE
Pres.: dūcī[2]
Perf.: ductus esse
Fut.: ductum īrī

[2]To form the present passive infinitive, replace the -ere of the active form with -ī.

SUPINE

ductum
ductū

GERUND

Nom.: dūcere
Gen.: dūcendī
Dat.: dūcendō
Acc.: dūcendum
Abl.: dūcendō

Fourth Conjugation

PRINCIPAL PARTS OF AUDIŌ

audiō	*I hear*	**audīvī**	*I have heard*
audīre	*to hear*	**audītus**	*having been heard*

INDICATIVE ACTIVE

Present	Perfect
audiō	audīvī
audīs	audīvistī
audit	audīvit
audīmus	audīvimus
audītis	audīvistis
audiunt	audīvērunt
Imperfect	*Pluperfect*
audiēbam	audīveram
audiēbās	audīverās
audiēbat	audīverat
audiēbāmus	audīverāmus
audiēbātis	audīverātis
audiēbant	audīverant
Future	*Future Perf.*
audiam	audīverō
audiēs	audīveris
audiet	audīverit
audiēmus	audīverimus
audiētis	audīveritis
audient	audīverint

INDICATIVE PASSIVE

Present	Perfect
audior	audītus, -a, -um **sum**
audīris	audītus, -a, -um **es**
audītur	audītus, -a, -um **est**
audīmur	audītī, -ae, -a **sumus**
audīminī	audītī, -ae, -a **estis**
audiuntur	audītī, -ae, -a **sunt**
Imperfect	*Pluperfect*
audiēbar	audītus, -a, -um **eram**
audiēbāris	audītus, -a, -um **erās**
audiēbātur	audītus, -a, -um **erat**
audiēbāmur	audītī, -ae, -a **erāmus**
audiēbāminī	audītī, -ae, -a **erātis**
audiēbantur	audītī, -ae, -a **erant**
Future	*Future Perfect*
audiar	audītus, -a, -um **erō**
audiēris	audītus, -a, -um **eris**
audiētur	audītus, -a, -um **erit**
audiēmur	audītī, -ae, -a **erimus**
audiēminī	audītī, -ae, -a **eritis**
audientur	audītī, -ae, -a **erunt**

SUBJUNCTIVE ACT.

Present	Perfect
audiam	audīverim
audiās	audīverīs
audiat	audīverit
audiāmus	audīverīmus
audiātis	audīverītis
audiant	audīverint
Imperfect	*Pluperfect*
audīrem	audīvissem
audīrēs	audīvissēs
audīret	audīvisset
audīrēmus	audīvissēmus
audīrētis	audīvissētis
audīrent	audīvissent

IMPERATIVE ACT.

Sing.: audī
Plur.: audīte

IMPERATIVE PASS.

Sing.: audīre
Plur.: audīminī

SUBJUNCTIVE PASSIVE

Present	Perfect
audiar	audītus, -a, -um **sim**
audiāris	audītus, -a, -um **sīs**
audiātur	audītus, -a, -um **sit**
audiāmur	audītī, -ae, -a **sīmus**
audiāminī	audītī, -ae, -a **sītis**
audiantur	audītī, -ae, -a **sint**
Imperfect	*Pluperfect*
audīrer	audītus, -a, -um **essem**
audīrēris	audītus, -a, -um **essēs**
audīrētur	audītus, -a, -um **esset**
audīrēmur	audītī, -ae, -a **essēmus**
audīrēminī	audītī, -ae, -a **essētis**
audīrentur	audītī, -ae, -a **essent**

PARTICIPLES

Present Active: audiēns
Perf. Passive: audītus, -a, -um
Fut. Active: audītūrus, -a, -um
Gerundive: audiendus, -a, -um

SUPINE

audītum, audītū

INFINITIVES[1]

ACTIVE
Pres.: audīre
Perf.: audīvisse
Fut.: audītūrus esse
PASSIVE
Pres.: audīrī
Perf.: audītus esse
Fut.: audītum īrī

[1]The present passive infinitive of the 1st, 2nd, and 4th conjugations is formed by replacing the final -e of the present active infin. with an ī.

GERUND

Nom.: audīre
Gen.: audiendī
Dat.: audiendō
Acc.: audiendum
Abl.: audiendō

2. ORTHOGRAPHIC-CHANGING AND IRREGULAR VERBS

The -io Verbs of the 3rd Conjugation

PRINCIPAL PARTS OF CAPIŌ

capiō	*I seize*	**cēpī**	*I have seized*
capere	*to seize*	**captus**	*having been seized*

INDICATIVE

The six tenses of the indicative active are conjugated like audiō (4th conjugation) except that the -i of capiō is short throughout the present tense.

In the indicative passive, the second person singular, present passive, differs from its parallel in audiō: caperis, audīris.

SUBJUNCTIVE

The imperfect subjunctive of capiō, both active and passive, is formed from the 2nd principal part, capere, while audiō performs the same way. For example:

ACTIVE		PASSIVE	
caperem	audīrem	caperer	audīrer
etc.	*etc.*	*etc.*	*etc.*

INFINITIVES

ACTIVE	
Pres.: capere	
Perf.: cēpisse	
Fut.: captūrus esse	
PASSIVE	
Pres.: capī	
Perf.: captus esse	
Fut.: captum īrī	

IMPERATIVE

ACTIVE	**PASSIVE**
cape	capere
capite	capiminī

GERUND AND SUPINE

These are formed like counterparts in audiō.

The Irregular Verb Sum

PRINCIPAL PARTS

sum	*I am*	**fuī**	*I have been*
esse	*to be*	**futūrus**	*being about to be*

INDICATIVE

Present	Perfect
sum	fuī
es	fuistī
est	fuit
sumus	fuimus
estis	fuistis
sunt	fuērunt
Imperf.	*Pluperf.*
eram	fueram
erās	fuerās
erat	fuerat
erāmus	fuerāmus
erātis	fuerātis
erant	fuerant
Future	*Fut. Perf.*
erō	fuerō
eris	fueris
erit	fuerit
erimus	fuerimus
eritis	fueritis
erunt	fuerint

SUBJUNCTIVE

Present	Perfect
sim	fuerim
sīs	fuerīs
sit	fuerit
sīmus	fuerīmus
sītis	fuerītis
sint	fuerint
Imperf.	*Pluperf.*
essem	fuissem
essēs	fuissēs
esset	fuisset
essēmus	fuissēmus
essētis	fuissētis
essent	fuissent

IMPERATIVE[1]

Present
es *be thou*
este *be ye*

[1]The future imperative of sum, esto, sometimes means *So be it.*

INFINITIVES

Present	Perfect
esse	fuisse
Future	
futūrus esse	

PARTICIPLE

Future
futūrus, -a, -um

The Irregular Verb Possum

PRINCIPAL PARTS

possum	*I am able*	**potuī**	*I have been able*
posse	*to be able*		

INDICATIVE

Present	Perfect
possum	potuī
potes	potuistī
potest	potuit
possumus	potuimus
potestis	potuistis
possunt	potuērunt
Imperfect	*Pluperf.*
poteram	potueram
poterās	potuerās
poterat	potuerat
poterāmus	potuerāmus
poterātis	potuerātis
poterant	potuerant
Future	*Fut. Perf.*
poterō	potuerō
poteris	potueris
poterit	potuerit
poterimus	potuerimus
poteritis	potueritis
poterunt	potuerint

SUBJUNCTIVE

Present	Perfect
possim	potuerim
possīs	potuerīs
possit	potuerit
possīmus	potuerīmus
possītis	potuerītis
possint	potuerint
Imperfect	*Pluperf.*
possem	potuissem
possēs	potuissēs
posset	potuisset
possēmus	potuissēmus
possētis	potuissētis
possent	potuissent

INFINITIVES

Present
posse
Perfect
potuisse

PARTICIPLE

Present
potēns (*Gen.* potentis)

Deponent Verbs (Passive in form; active in meaning)

There are deponent verbs in all four conjugations. All are regularly passive in form. Exceptions are the future infinitive and the present and future participles, which are active in form (see cōnor, on the right).

cōnāns — *trying* (1st conjug.)
cōnātus — *having tried*
cōnātūrus — *being about to try*
cōnandus — *worthy to be tried*

Present: cōnarī — *to try*
Perfect: cōnātus esse — *to have tried*
Future: cōnātūrus esse — *to be about to try*

The Irregular Verb Ferō

PRINCIPAL PARTS

ferō	*I bear*	**tulī**	*I have borne*
ferre	*to bear*	**lātus**	*having been borne*

INDICATIVE ACTIVE

Present	Perfect
ferō	tulī
fers	tulistī
fert	tulit
ferimus	tulimus
fertis	tulistis
ferunt	tulērunt
Imperf.	*Pluperf.*
ferēbam	tuleram
ferēbās	tulerās
ferēbat	tulerat
etc.	*etc.*
Future	*Fut. Perf.*
feram	tulerō
ferēs	tuleris
feret	tulerit
etc.	*etc.*

INDICATIVE PASSIVE

Present	Perfect
feror	lātus, -a, -um **sum**
ferris	lātus, -a, -um **es**
fertur	lātus, -a, -um **est**
ferimur	*etc.*
feriminī	
feruntur	
Imperf.	*Pluperfect*
ferēbar	lātus, -a, -um **eram**
ferēbāris	lātus, -a, -um **erās**
ferēbātur	lātus, -a, -um **erat**
etc.	*etc.*
Future	*Future Perfect*
ferar	lātus, -a, -um **erō**
ferēris	lātus, -a, -um **eris**
ferētur	lātus, -a, -um **erit**
etc.	*etc.*

SUBJUNCTIVE ACTIVE

Present	Perfect
feram	tulerim
ferās	tuleris
ferat	tulerit
etc.	*etc.*
Imperf.	*Pluperf.*
ferrem	tulissem
ferrēs	tulissēs
ferret	tulisset
etc.	*etc.*

SUBJUNCTIVE PASSIVE

Present	Perfect
ferar	lātus, -a, -um **sim**
ferāris	lātus, -a, -um **sīs**
ferātur	lātus, -a, -um **sit**
etc.	*etc.*
Imperf.	*Pluperfect*
ferrer	lātus, -a, -um **essem**
ferrēris	lātus, -a, -um **essēs**
ferrētur	lātus, -a, -um **esset**
etc.	*etc.*

IMPERATIVE ACTIVE

Present
Sing.: fer
Plur.: ferte

INFINITIVES—ACTIVE

Present
ferre
Perfect
tulisse
Future
lātūrus esse

PARTICIPLES—ACTIVE

Present
ferēns
Future
lātūrus, -a, -um

IMPERATIVE—PASSIVE

Present
Sing.: ferre
Plur.: feriminī

INFINITIVES—PASSIVE

Present
ferrī
Perfect
lātus esse
Future
lātum īrī

PARTICIPLES—PASSIVE

Perfect
lātus, -a, -um
Gerundive
ferendus, -a, -um

SUPINE
lātum
lātū

GERUND
Nom.: ferre   *Acc.:* ferend**um**
Gen.: ferendī   *Abl.:* ferend**ō**
Dat.: ferendō

The Irregular Verbs Volō, Nōlō, and Mālō

Nōlō is made up from nē-volō, while mālō is curtailed from magis-volō.

PRINCIPAL PARTS

volō	*I wish*
velle	*to wish*
voluī	*I have wished*

Note: With the exception of the present tense, the forms of nōlō and mālō are similar to volō. For forms not given below, see volō, which is complete.

INDICATIVE

Present	Perfect
volō	voluī
vīs	voluistī
vult	voluit
volumus	voluimus
vultis	voluistis
volunt	voluērunt
Imperfect	*Pluperfect*
volēbam	volueram
volēbās	voluerās
volēbat	voluerat
volēbāmus	voluerāmus
volēbātis	voluerātis
volēbant	voluerant
Future	*Future Perf.*
volam	voluerō
volēs	volueris
volet	voluerit
volēmus	voluerimus
volētis	volueritis
volent	voluerint

IMPERATIVE
(none)

INFINITIVES
Present: velle
Perfect: voluisse

PARTICIPLES
Present: volēns
(Gen. volentis)

SUBJUNCTIVE

Present	Perfect
velim	voluerim
velīs	voluerīs
velit	voluerit
velīmus	voluerīmus
velītis	voluerītis
velint	voluerint
Imperfect	*Pluperfect*
vellem	voluissem
vellēs	voluissēs
vellet	voluisset
vellēmus	voluissēmus
vellētis	voluissētis
vellent	voluissent

PRINCIPAL PARTS

mālō	*I prefer*
mālle	*to prefer*
māluī	*I have prefered*

INDIC.	SUBJ.
Present	*Present*
mālō	mālim
māvīs	mālīs
māvult	mālit
mālumus	mālīmus
māvultis	mālītis
mālunt	mālint

INFINITIVES
mālle
māluisse

PRINCIPAL PARTS

nōlō	*I do not wish*
nōlle	*to be unwilling*
nōluī	*I have been unwilling*

INDICATIVE	SUBJUNCTIVE
Present	*Present*
nōlō	nōlim
nōn vīs	nōlīs
nōn vult	nōlit
nōlumus	nōlīmus
nōn vultis	nōlītis
nōlunt	nōlint

IMPERATIVE[1]
Sing.: nōlī
Plur.: nōlīte

(These forms, plus a complementary infinitive, express a negative command.)

[1]Mālō and volō do not have imperative forms. Mālō is deficient in participles also.

INFINITIVES
nōlle
nōluisse

PARTICIPLES
nōlēns
nōlentis (*Gen.*)

The Irregular Verb Fiō

PRINCIPAL PARTS

fīō	*I am made*
fierī	*to be made*
factus	*having been made*

Note: Fīō is the irregular passive of faciō. Even though it is conjugated actively in the present, future, imperfect, it always has passive meaning.

INDICATIVE

Present	Perfect 1
fīō	factus, -a, -um **sum**
fīs	*etc.*
fit	
fīmus	
fītis	
fīunt	
Imperf.	*Pluperfect*
fīēbam	factus, -a, -um **eram**
fīēbās	*etc.*
fīēbat	
fīēbāmus	
fīēbātis	
fīēbant	
Future	*Future Perfect*
fīam	factus, -a, -um **erō**
fīēs	*etc.*
fīet	
fīēmus	
fīētis	
fīent	

PARTICIPLES
Present: (none)
Perfect: factus
Gerundive: faciendus

SUBJUNCTIVE

Present	Perfect
fīam	factus, -a, -um **sim**
fīās	*etc.*
fīat	
fīāmus	
fīātis	
fīant	
Imperf.	*Pluperfect*
fierem	factus, -a, -um **essem**
fierēs	*etc.*
fieret	
fierēmus	
fierētis	
fierent	

[1]Most compounds of faciō become -ficiō, while factus becomes -fectus. They are conjugated ike capiō. *But* the passive of satisfaciō is satisfīō.

INFINITIVES
Present: fierī
Perfect: factus esse
Future: factum īrī

The Irregular Verb eō[1]

PRINCIPAL PARTS

eō	*I go*	iī (īvī)	*I have gone*
īre	*to go*	itum (est)	*it has been gone*

INDICATIVE

Present	Future	Pluperf.
eō	ībō	ieram
īs	ībis	ierās
it	ībit	ierat
īmus	ībimus	ierāmus
ītis	ībitis	ierātis
eunt	ībunt	ierant
Imperf.	*Perfect*	*Fut. Perf.*
ībam	iī	ierō
ībās	iistī	ieris
ībat	iit	ierit
ībāmus	iimus	ierimus
ībātis	iistis	ieritis
ībant	iērunt	ierint

PARTICIPLES
Present: iēns (euntis)
Future: itūrus, -a, -um
Gerundive: eundus

SUBJUNCTIVE

Present	Perfect
eam	ierim
eās	ierīs
eat	ierit
eāmus	ierīmus
eātis	ierītis
eant	ierint
Imperf.	*Pluperfect*
īrem	iissem (īssem)
īrēs	iissēs
īret	iisset
īrēmus	iissēmus
īrētis	iissētis
īrent	iissent

IMPERATIVE

Present
Sing.: ī
Plur.: īte

INFINITIVES
Pres.: īre
Perf.: iisse
Fut.: itūrus esse

GERUND
Nom.: īre
Gen.: eundī
Dat.: eundō
Acc.: eund**um**
Abl.: eund**ō**

SUPINE
itum — *to go*
itū — *to go*

The Defective Verbs Coepī, Ōdī, and Meminī

These verbs have forms in the perfect system only, the present, imperfect, and future tenses having been displaced. Coepī is the only one of the three to have passive forms; the other two are conjugated only in the perfect active systems. The conjugations of all three are otherwise perfectly regular and have not been reproduced below.

PRINCIPAL PARTS	**INFINITIVES**	**PARTICIPLES**
coepī — *I began* [1]	*Perfect*	*Perfect*
coepisse — *to have begun*	coepisse	coeptus
coeptus — *begun*	*Future*	*Future*
(Note *past* meaning.)	coeptūrus esse	coeptūrus
ōdī — *I hate*	*Perfect:* ōdisse	*Perfect:* ōsus
ōdisse — *to hate*	*Future:* ōsūrus esse	*Future:* ōsūrus
ōsus — *hated, hating*		
(Note *present* meaning.)		

Ōdī lacks imperatives.

meminī — *I remember*	*Perfect:* meminisse	**IMPERATIVE**
meminisse — *to remember*		*Sing.:* mementō
(Note *present* meaning.)		*Plur.:* mementōte

[1]Adeō, ineō, and trānseō are transitive and may therefore be conjugated in the passive. Queō and nequeō are conjugated like eō.

[1]For a present meaning of *"begin,"* use incipiō. Coepī has no imperative forms.

3. SYNTAX OF VERBS

Indicative Mood

1. The historical present is used to make the past more vivid: Mīlitēs iter **faciunt.** *The soldiers made a journey.*
2. **Iam** with any expression of time, plus the present, equals the English perfect: **Iam diū** in Americā **est.** *He has been.* **Iam** plus the imperfect equals the English pluperfect: Iam multōs annōs **rēgnābat.** *He had been...*
3. **Dum** *(while)* plus the present equals the English past. **Dum pugnant,** imperātor pervēnit. *While they were fighting...*
4. **Quamquam** and **etsī** *(although)* take any tense of the indicative: **Quamquam** Rōmae est... *Although he is in Rome...*
5. **Postquam** *(after)*, **ubi** *(when)*, **simul atque** *(as soon as)*, plus the Latin perfect, equal English pluperfect: **Postquam** ad oppidum **pervēnit...** *After he had arrived at the town...*
6. Causal clauses introduced by **quod** or **quoniam** employ the indicative: Fortissimī sunt illī virī **quod** longissimē **absunt.** *Those men are the bravest because they are the farthest in.*
7. Temporal clauses introduced by **cum** and showing true time are in the indicative: Tum **cum** multī rēs magnās **āmīserant...** *At the time when many men had lost great fortunes...*
8. Relative clauses are usually in the indicative: ...in partēs trēs, quārum ūnam **incolunt** Belgae *...into three parts, of which the Belgians inhabit one.* (For relative clauses in subjunctive, see below.)

Subjunctive Mood—Independent Uses

1. Deliberative or dubitative questions (rhetorical or expressing doubt) use the subjunctive: Quid **agam,** iūdicēs? *What am I to do, jurors?*
2. Statements of potential (possible action) employ subjunctive: **Dīcat** quispiam... *Someone may say...*
3. Commands of the 1st or 3rd person are in subjunctive (hortatory subjunctive): **Laudēmus...** *Let us praise...* **Laudet...** *Let him praise...* (BUT 2nd person commands are in imperative: **Laudā...** *(You) Praise...*)
4. Wishes possible of fulfillment are in present subjunctive: Utinam **vīvat!** *Oh that he might live (go on living)!* Wishes impossible of fulfillment are in imperfect or pluperfect subjunctive: Utinam **vīveret!** *If he were only alive!*
5. Conditional ("if-then") sentences possible of fulfillment employ present subjunctive in both clauses: Sī pater tēcum **loquātur,** nōnne audīre **debeās?** *If your father speaks, shouldn't you listen?*
6. Conditional sentences impossible of fulfillment (or contrary to fact) employ the imperfect subjunctive or the pluperfect subjunctive: Sī hoc **accidisset,** Clōdius nōn mortuus **esset.** *If this had happened, Clōdius would not have died.*

Some Special Verb Rules

1. A finite verb agrees with its subject in person and number.
2. A question expecting the answer "maybe" has the suffix **-ne** attached to the most important word in the sentence. A question introduced by **nōnne** expects "yes;" **num** expects "no."
3. Verbs meaning *favor, help, please, trust* (and their opposites) and *believe, persuade, command, obey, serve, resist, envy, pardon,* and *spare* take the dative case.
4. Many Verbs compounded with **ad, ante, con, in, inter, ob, post, prae, prō, sub,** and **super** take the dative case.
5. The direct object of a transitive verb is in the accusative case.
6. The subject of an infinitive is in the accusative case.
7. The deponent verbs, **ūtor, fruor, fungor, potior, vēscor** take the ablative case.
8. Verbs of fearing take the subjunctive with **nē** *(that)* and **ut** or **nē nōn** *(that not).*
9. Attraction means that a verb ordinarily indicative is attracted into the subjunctive mood by the proximity of another subjunctive.

Subjunctive Mood—Dependent Uses

1. Any subordinate clause introduced by an interrogative word is an indirect question. It ordinarily depends upon a verb of *knowing, telling, seeing, hearing,* or any expression of uncertainty. The verb of the indirect question goes in the subjunctive. The tense of the subjunctive clause depends upon whether the action of the indicative verb in the main clause is continuing or complete. There are two sequences of tenses (depending upon the two possible times of the main verb):
   A. Primary (main verb in present time):
      Scit quid **faciam.** *He knows what I am doing.*
      Scit quid **factūrus sim.**[1] *He knows what I shall do.*
      Scit quid **fēcerim.** *He knows what I did.*
   B. Secondary (main verb in past time):
      Scīvit quid **facerem.** *He knew what I was doing.*
      Scīvit quid **factūrus essem.**[1] *He knew what I was going to do.*
      Scīvit quid **fēcissem.** *He knew what I had done.*

[1]Since in this instance a future form of the subjunctive is needed, the present and imperfect forms of the verb **sum** are used, along with the future participle, to take the place of the missing form.

2. Purpose Clauses — Adverbial. The purpose clause modifies the introducing verb. Venit ut mē **videat.** *He comes to (literally, in order that he may) see me.*
3. Purpose Clauses — Relative. The purpose clause is adjectival. Mīsit explōrātōrem quī mīlitēs **dūceret.** *He sent a scout to lead the soldiers.*
4. Purpose Clauses — Substantive. The clause is the object of a verb of asking, commanding, etc. Eīs persuādēbit ut **exeant.** *He will persuade them to leave.*
5. Result Clauses — Adverbial. Tam fortis erat ut vincī nōn **posset.** *He was so brave that he could not be conquered.*
6. Result Clauses — Substantive. Accidit ut **sit** lūna plēna. *It happens that the moon is full.*
7. After verbs of fearing. Germānī verēbantur nē Caesar cōpiās trāns Rhēnum **trādūceret.** *The Germans feared that Caesar would lead troops across the Rhine.* Note: After verbs of fearing, **nē** replaces **ut,** and **ut** becomes negative "that not."
8. In **Cum** Clauses (when **cum** means *when, since,* or *although).* Cum id **nūntiātum esset...** *When this was announced...* Quae cum ita **sint...** *Since this is so...* Cum prīmī ōrdinēs **concidissent...** *Although the first ranks had fallen...*
9. After **Dum** (meaning *until).* Dum relīquae nāvēs **convenīrent,** ad nōnam hōram exspectāvit. *He waited until (to) the ninth hour, until the rest of the ships would assemble.*
10. Clauses of comparison introduced by **utsi, velutsi, quasi.** Dīcit velutsi **sit** āmēns. *He speaks as if he were mad.*
11. Negative expressions of doubt and hindering: Nōn est dubium quīn mīlitēs **sint** fortēs. *There is no doubt that the soldiers are brave.*
12. Relative Clause of Description — Erat mīles quī fortiter **pugnāret.** *He was a soldier who would fight bravely.*

Syntax of the Infinitive

1. In indirect statement when the statement made by a speaker is reported by someone, the subject is in the accusative case, the verb becomes an infinitive, and any subordinate verb becomes subjunctive. In deciding upon the tense of any subordinate verb, the sequence of tenses is followed. In deciding upon the tense of the infinitive, the problem may be resolved by returning the sentence to direct statement, and then using the same tense of the infinitive.
   Dīcit sē **venīre.** *He says that he is coming.* (direct: *I am coming.*)
   Dīxit sē **venīre.** *He said that he was coming.* (direct: *I am coming.*)
   Dīcit sē **vēnisse.** *He says that he has come.* (direct: *I have come.*)
   Dīxit sē **vēnisse.** *He said that he had come.* (direct: *I have come.*)
   Dīcit sē **ventūrum esse.** *He says that he will come.* (direct: *I shall come.*)
   Dīxit sē **ventūrum esse.** *He said that he would come.* (direct: *I shall come.*)
   Subordinate clauses occurring within an indirect statement are often conditions. In such cases, the "if clause" is in the subjunctive and the "conclusion" is an infinitive construction. Dīxit sī īret, nēminem secūtūrum **esse.** *He said that if he should go, no one should follow.*
2. Complementary Infinitive. An infinitive without a subject is used to complete the action of certain verbs:

possum — *I am able*	statuō — *I determine*
volō — *I wish*	cōnor — *I try*
nōlō — *I do not wish*	temptō — *I try*
mālō — *I prefer*	audeō — *I dare*
cupiō — *I desire*	dēbeō — *I ought*
patior — *I allow*	constituō — *I decide*
dubitō — *I hesitate*	parō — *I prepare*
incipiō — *I begin*	dēsistō — *I cease*
	videor — *I seem*

   Bellum **īnferre** possunt... *They are able to make war on...*
3. Objective Infinitive. Many verbs which ordinarily would take a complementary infinitive take an objective infinitive when the subject of the verb is different from the subject of the infinitive. Eum **abīre** iussērunt. *They ordered him to go away.*
4. Subjective Infinitive. Facile est hoc **facere.** *To do this is easy.*
5. Historical Infinitive. The infinitive, with a nominative subject, is sometimes used to express past time more vividly. Ego **īnstāre** ut mihi respondēret. *I kept urging him to reply to me.*

Syntax of Participles

1. Participles are verbals which perform as adjectives. Mīlitēs **moritūrī** proelium commīsērunt. *The soldiers who were about to die engaged in battle.*
2. Future passive participles (sometimes called gerundives) express necessity or obligation. Vir **laudandus.** *A man worthy to be praised.* The future passive participle used with some form of sum is called the second periphrastic conjugation. Puella **est amanda.** *The girl ought to be loved.*
3. The future active participle combined with sum (first periphrastic conjugation) is a way of expressing futurity, even in past time. Ducem **monitūrus eram.** *I was about to advise the general.*
4. The gerund is a verbal noun which is declinable only in the singular. The gerund, as a verb, may take an object. Ars bene **disserendī...** *The art of speaking well...*
5. The supine, ending in **-um,** is used to express purpose with verbs of motion. **Pugnātum** vēnērunt. *They came to fight.* Ending in **-ū,** the supine is used with certain adjectives. Difficile **factū...** *Difficult to do...*

Nouns are the names of persons, places, or things. In Latin, nouns, pronouns, and adjectives are inflected to show their grammatical relations to the other words in the sentence. These inflectional endings are usually equivalent to prepositional phrases in English.

The names of the cases and their functions are as follows:

LATIN CASE	USE IN THE SENTENCE	ENGLISH CASE	EXAMPLE
Nominative	Subject or subj. complement.	Nominative.	Puer *(the or a boy)*
Genitive	Shows possession and other relationships.	Possessive or the objective, with "of."	Puerī *(of the boy, or of a boy)*
Dative	Indirect object and other relationships.	Objective, often with "to" or "for."	Puerō *(to or for the boy)*
Accusative	Direct object.	Objective.	Puerum *(boy, or the boy)*
Ablative	Occurs in adverbial phrases, usually with a preposition.	Objective, as object of many prepositions.	Puerō *(by the boy, from, with, on, at, etc.)*

There are two additional cases which occur infrequently, and are not usually given with the declensions:

Vocative	Case of address. (The Latin inflectional ending is the same as in the nominative with exceptions noted, p. 7.)	Nominative of address.	Puer! *(Boy!)*
Locative	Case of "place at which," with cities, towns, small islands, and **domus** *(home)* only.	Objective, with "at."	Rōmae *(at Rome)*

Inflection in General

The inflectional ending of a word shows its *number, gender,* and *case*. The general concepts of number and case are similar to their counterparts in English (singular-plural, case structure outlined above). However, *gender* in Latin is often *grammatical* only, and unrelated to *natural* gender. Although there are the same three genders (masculine, feminine, neuter) in Latin as in English, it is not uncommon for a word like nauta *(sailor)*, which is naturally male, to appear in a feminine declension (1st declension). Inflected words are comprised of two parts: the *base* and the inflected portion. The *base* is that part of the word which remains unchanged, and the base of any noun may be determined by removing the ending of the *genitive singular* form. The base of **terra** is **terr-**; the base of **ager** is **agr-**, and so on.

4. NOUNS
First and Second Declension Nouns

The gender of most 1st declension nouns is feminine. That of most 2nd declension nouns is neuter (ending in **-um**) or masculine (ending in **-us** or **-er**).

	1st Declension — Fem.		2nd Declension — Masc.		2nd Declension — Neut.		2nd Declension Masc. Ending in -er			
	Sing.	*Plur.*	*Sing.*	*Plur.*	*Sing.*	*Plur.*	*Sing.*	*Plur.*	*Sing.*	*Plur.*
Nom.	terra *(land)*	-ae	dominus *(lord)*	-ī	cael**um** *(sky)*	-a	ager *(field)*	agrī	puer *(boy)*	-ī
Gen.	terrae	-ārum	dominī	-ōrum	caelī	-ōrum	agrī	-ōrum	puerī	-ōrum
Dat.	terrae	-īs	dominō	-īs	caelō	-īs	agrō	-īs	puerō	-īs
Acc.	terram	-ās	domin**um**	-ōs	cael**um**	-a	agrum	-ōs	puerum	-ōs
Abl.	terrā	-īs	dominō	-īs	caelō	-īs	agrō	-īs	puerō	-īs

Third Declension Nouns

The trademark of the 3rd declension is the ending **-is** in the genitive singular. It is added to the base. All genders are represented in the 3rd declension.[1]

	(light)		*(soldier)*		*(ship)*		*(night)*		*(sea)*		*(type)*		*(river)*	
	Sing.	*Plur.*	*Sing.*	*Plur.*	*Sing.*	*Plur.*	*Sing.*	*Plur.*	*Sing.*	*Plur.*	*Sing.*	*Plur.*	*Sing.*	*Plur.*
Nom.	lūx	lūcēs	mīles	mīlitēs	nāvis	-ēs	nox	noctēs	mare	-ia	genus	genera	flūmen	flūmina
Gen.	lūcis	-um	mīlitis	-um	nāvis	-ium	noctis	-ium	maris	-ium	generis	-um	flūminis	-um
Dat.	lūcī	-ibus	mīlitī	-ibus	nāvī	-ibus	noctī	-ibus	marī	-ibus	generī	-ibus	flūminī	-ibus
Acc.	lūcem	-ēs	mīlitem	-ēs	nāvem	-ēs (-īs)	noctem	-ēs (-īs)	mare	-ia	genus	-a	flūmen	-a
Abl.	lūce	-ibus	mīlite	-ibus	nāve	-ibus	nocte	-ibus	marī	-ibus	genere	-ibus	flūmine	-ibus

[1] Nouns ending in **-is** or **-es** that have the same number of syllables in the genitive and the nominative take **-ium** in the genitive plural and, sometimes, **-īs** in the accusative plural.

Nouns whose bases end in double consonants take **-ium** in the genitive plural and, sometimes, **-īs** in the accusative plural.

Neuter nouns ending in **-e, -al,** or **-ar** take **-ī** in the ablative singular, **-ia** in the nominative and accusative plural, and **-ium** in the genitive plural.

Irregular Nouns of the Third Declension

A. Bōs, bovis *(ox, cow)* has **boum** in the genitive plural and **bōbus** or **būbus** in the dative and ablative plural.
B. Carō, carnis *(flesh)*, fem., has **carnium** in the genitive plural.
C. Vīs *(force in sing., strength in plur.)*, fem., is declined **vīs, vis, vī, vim, vī, (plur.) vīrēs, vīrium, vīribus, vīrēs (-īs), vīribus.**
D. Turris, turris *(tower)*, fem., and sitis, sitis *(thirst)*, fem., have **-im** in the accusative singular, and **-ī** in the ablative singular.
E. Senex, senis *(old man)*, masc., has **senum** in the genitive plural.

F. Sus, suis *(swine)*, masc. and fem., has **suum** in the genitive plural, and **subus** (suibus) in the dative and ablative plural.
G. The declension of Iuppiter *(Jupiter):* **Iuppiter, Iovis, Iovī, Iovem, Iove.**
H. Iter, itineris *(route, march, journey)*, neuter.
I. Hērōs, hērōis, hērōī, hērōa, hērōe is a Greek masc. noun meaning *hero*.
J. Ilias, Iliados *(The Iliad)*, fem., is declined like hērōs.

Fourth Declension Nouns

Most fourth declension nouns are masculine and are formed from the 4th principal part of the verb. Feminine nouns of the 4th declension are: **anus** *(old woman)*, **manus** *(hand)*, **domus** *(house)*, **tribus** *(tribe)*. There are also a few names of trees, such as **pinus** *(pine)* and **ficus** *(fig)*. There are very few neuters in the 4th declension; **cornū** *(horn)* and **pecū** *(cattle)* are two. The ending **-ubus** sometimes replaces **-ibus** in the dative and ablative plural; **tribus** and **lacus** *(lake)* are common examples.

	Masc. *(port)*		Fem. *(house)*		Neut. *(knee)*	
	Sing.	*Plur.*	*Sing.*	*Plur.*	*Sing.*	*Plur.*
Nom.	portus	-ūs	domus	-ūs	genū	-ua
Gen.	portūs	-uum	domūs (-ī)	-uum (-ōrum)	genūs	-uum
Dat.	portuī (-ū)	-ibus	domuī (-ō)	-ibus	genū	-ibus
Acc.	portum	-ūs	domum	-ōs (-ūs)	genū	-ua
Abl.	portū	-ibus	domō (-ū)	-ibus	genū	-ibus

Note: Domus has forms in both 2nd and 4th declensions.

Fifth Declension Nouns

Only 3 nouns in the 5th declension are declined throughout: **diēs, rēs,** and **merīdiēs** *(noon, south).*
The following are used in the singular throughout, but only in the nominative and the accusative plural: **aciēs** *(sharp edge, line of battle)*, **effigiēs** *(likeness)*, **faciēs** *(face)*, **glaciēs** *(ice)*, **seriēs** *(series, succession)*, **speciēs** *(appearance)*, and **spēs** *(hope).*

All 5th declension nouns are feminine except diēs, which is occasionally feminine, and merīdiēs, which is masculine.

	Sing.	*Plur.*	*Sing.*	*Plur.*
Nom.	diēs *(day)*	diēs	rēs *(matter)*	rēs
Gen.	diēī	-ērum	reī	rērum
Dat.	diēī	-ēbus	reī	rēbus
Acc.	diem	-ēs	rem	rēs
Abl.	diē	-ēbus	rē	rēbus

Defective Nouns

Many Latin nouns are defective in case. Outstanding are nouns having only two cases: **fors**, nominative *(chance)*, **forte**, ablative *(by chance)*; and **spontis**, genitive *(accord)*, **sponte**, ablative *(of one's accord)*. Other nouns are defective in number. These nouns are used only in the plural: **arma, armōrum**, neut. *(arms)*; **castra, castrōrum**, neut. *(camp)*; **Kalendae, Kalendārum**, fem. *(The Kalends)*; **īnsidiae, īnsidiārum**, fem. *(ambush)*; **īnferī, -ōrum**, masc. *(the dead, the underworld).*

5. ADJECTIVES
First and Second Declension Adjectives

Adjectives agree with their nouns in gender, number, and case. Those in the predicate after **sum** *(be)* agree with the subject, as in English. Most masculine adjectives are declined like ager, puer, or dominus, neuter adjectives like caelum, and feminine adjectives like terra.

	Masculine		Feminine		Neuter	
	Sing.	*Plur.*	*Sing.*	*Plur.*	*Sing.*	*Plur.*
Nom.	bonus	-ī	bona	-ae	bonum	-a
Gen.	bonī	-ōrum	bonae	-ārum	bonī	-ōrum
Dat.	bonō	-īs	bonae	-īs	bonō	-īs
Acc.	bonum	-ōs	bonam	-ās	bonum	-a
Abl.	bonō	-īs	bonā	-īs	bonō	-īs

Third Declension Adjectives

Third declension adjectives fall into four distinct categories: (1) *three-termination*, with separate endings for all three genders, like **ācer**; (2) *two-termination*, with the same endings for masculine and feminine, like **omnis**; (3) *one-termination*, with the nominative singular the same in all genders, like **potēns**; and (4) the *comparative* of all adjectives, like **longior**. Present participles are declined like **potēns**.

(1) ācer (keen)

	Masc. Sing.	Masc. Plur.	Fem. Sing.	Fem. Plur.	Neut. Sing.	Neut. Plur.
Nom.	ācer	ācrēs	ācris	ācrēs	ācre	ācria
Gen.	ācris	-ium	ācris	-ium	ācris	-ium
Dat.	ācrī	-ibus	ācrī	-ibus	ācrī	-ibus
Acc.	ācrem	-ēs (-īs)	ācrem	-ēs (-īs)	ācre	-ia
Abl.	ācrī	-ibus	ācrī	-ibus	ācrī	-ibus

(2) omnis (all)

	Masc. & Fem. Sing.	Masc. & Fem. Plur.	Neut. Sing.	Neut. Plur.
Nom.	omnis	-ēs	omne	-ia
Gen.	omnis	-ium	omnis	-ium
Dat.	omnī	-ibus	omnī	-ibus
Acc.	omnem	-ēs (-īs)	omne	-ia
Abl.	omnī	-ibus	omnī	-ibus

(3) potēns (powerful)

	Masc. & Fem. Sing.	Masc. & Fem. Plur.	Neut. Sing.	Neut. Plur.
Nom.	potēns	potentēs	potēns	potentia
Gen.	potentis	-ium	potentis	-ium
Dat.	potentī	-ibus	potentī	-ibus
Acc.	potentem	-ēs (-īs)	potēns	-ia
Abl.	potentī (-e)	-ibus	potentī (-e)	-ibus

(4) longior (longer)

	Masc. & Fem. Sing.	Masc. & Fem. Plur.	Neut. Sing.	Neut. Plur.
Nom.	longior	longiōrēs	longius	longiōra
Gen.	longiōris	-um	longiōris	-um
Dat.	longiōrī	-ibus	longiōrī	-ibus
Acc.	longiōrem	-ēs (-īs)	longius	-a
Abl.	longiōre	-ibus	longiōre	-ibus

(5) plūs (more)

	Masc. & Fem. Sing.	Masc. & Fem. Plur.	Neut. Sing.	Neut. Plur.
Nom.		plūrēs	plūs	plūra
Gen.		-ium	plūris	-ium
Dat.		-ibus	plūrī	-ibus
Acc.		-ēs (-īs)	plūs	-a
Abl.		-ibus	plūre	-ibus

The Nine Irregular Adjectives

There are nine adjectives ("the naughty nine") which are regular in the plural and irregular in the singular. The plurals of these words are declined like **bonus**. With the exceptions noted, the *singulars* of these adjectives are declined like **tōtus**.

tōtus (whole, all)

alius	*other, another*	alter	*the other*
	(neut. — aliud)		(gen. — alterīus)
ūllus	*any*	nūllus	*no, none*
ūnus	*one, alone*	sōlus	*alone, only*
neuter	*neither*	uter	*which of two*
	(gen. — neutrīus)		(gen. — utrīus)

	Masc.	Fem.	Neut.
Nom.	tōtus	tōta	tōtum
Gen.	tōtīus	tōtīus	tōtīus
Dat.	tōtī	tōtī	tōtī
Acc.	tōtum	tōtam	tōtum
Abl.	tōtō	tōtā	tōtō

Comparison of Adjectives

There are three degrees of comparison in Latin, just as there are in English: *positive, comparative,* and *superlative*. The *comparative* is formed by adding **-ior** for the masculine and feminine, and **-ius** for the neuter to the base of the *positive*. The *superlative* is formed by adding **-issimus, -a, -um** to the base. The *comparative* is declined like **longior** on page 6 of this chart; the *positive* is declined like bonus for 1st and 2nd declension, like omnis for third declension adjectives. The *superlative* is declined like bonus.

REGULAR FORMS

Positive	Comparative	Superlative
longus, -a, -um	long**ior**, longius	long**issimus**, -a, -um
fortis, forte	fort**ior**, fortius	fort**issimus**, -a, -um

Note: Six adjectives ending in **-lis** (facilis, difficilis, similis, dissimilis, gracilis, humilis) add **-limus** instead of -issimus to the base to form the *superlative*. (facilis, facilior, facillimus.)

Note: Adjectives ending in **-er** add **-rimus** instead of -issimus to form the *superlative*.

miser, -a, -um	miserior, miserius	miserrimus, -a, -um
ācer, -is, -e	ācrior, ācrius	ācerrimus, -a, -um

IRREGULAR COMPARISONS

Positive	Comparative	Superlative
bonus *(good)*	melior	optimus
malus *(bad)*	peior	pessimus
magnus *(large)*	maior	maximus
multus *(much)*	plūs	plūrimus
multī *(many)*	plūrēs	plūrimī
parvus *(small)*	minor	minimus
maledicus *(slanderous)*	maledicentior	maledicentissimus
malevolus *(spiteful)*	malevolentior	malevolentissimus

Note: Adjectives ending in **-ius** or **-eus** add **magis** to form the comparative and **maximē** to form the superlative: idōneus, magis idōneus, maximē idōneus.

6. PRONOUNS

Pronouns, as the name implies, take the place of nouns. At times, they are used as adjectives, to modify nouns. Under those circumstances, they agree with the nouns in gender, number, and case.

Personal Pronouns

1st Person

	Sing.		Plur.	
Nom.	ego	*I*	nōs	*we*
Gen.	meī	*of me*	nostrum, nostrī	*of us*
Dat.	mihi	*to me*	nōbīs	*to us*
Acc.	mē	*me*	nōs	*us*
Abl.	mē	*by, etc., me*	nōbīs	*by, etc., us*

2nd Person

	Sing.		Plur.	
Nom.	tū	*you*	vōs	*you*
Gen.	tuī	*of you*	vestrum, vestrī	*of you*
Dat.	tibi	*to you*	vōbīs	*to you*
Acc.	tē	*you*	vōs	*you*
Abl.	tē	*by, etc., you*	vōbīs	*by, etc., you*

3rd Person: A demonstrative pronoun is used as the pronoun of the 3rd person.

The Demonstrative Pronouns (or Adjectives)

There are 5 demonstratives used to point out special objects or persons.
Hic *(this here)* refers to what is near the speaker in place, time, or thought. Sometimes the word may also mean *he, she, or it.*
Ille *(that there)* refers to something remote from the speaker. It also means *that famous.*
Is, ea, id are most commonly used for *he, she,* or *it.* They may also mean *this or that.*
Iste *(that — nearby* or *that of yours)* is often used comtemptuously.
Īdem means *the same.*

Masc.	Fem.	Neut.	Masc.	Fem.	Neut.
hic	haec	hoc	ille	illa	illud
huius	huius	huius	illīus	illīus	illīus
huic	huic	huic	illī	illī	illī
hunc	hanc	hoc	illum	illam	illud
hōc	hāc	hōc	illō	illā	illō
hī	hae	haec	illī	illae	illa
hōrum	hārum	hōrum	illōrum	illārum	illōrum
hīs	hīs	hīs	illīs	illīs	illīs
hōs	hās	haec	illōs	illās	illa
hīs	hīs	hīs	illīs	illīs	illīs

Masc.	Fem.	Neut.	Masc.	Fem.	Neut.
is	ea	id	iste	ista	istud
ēius	ēius	ēius	istīus	istīus	istīus
eī	eī	eī	istī	istī	istī
eum	eam	id	istum	istam	istud
eō	eā	eō	istō	istā	istō
eī	eae	ea	istī	istae	ista
eōrum	eārum	eōrum	istōrum	istārum	istōrum
eīs	eīs	eīs	istīs	istīs	istīs
eōs	eās	ea	istōs	istās	ista
eīs	eīs	eīs	istīs	istīs	istīs

Masc.	Fem.	Neut.
īdem	eadem	idem
ēiusdem	ēiusdem	ēiusdem
eīdem	eīdem	eīdem
eundem	eandem	idem
eōdem	eādem	eōdem
eīdem	eaedem	eadem
eōrundem	eārundem	eōrundem
eīsdem	eīsdem	eīsdem
eōsdem	eāsdem	eadem
eīsdem	eīsdem	eīsdem

Indefinite Pronouns

Quis, quispiam, aliquis, and **quīdam** are the indefinite pronouns. **Quis** is usually used immediately after sī, nisi, nē, and num. Only the quis and quī of the indefinites may be declined: **quis** is declined like the interrogative below; **quī** is declined like the relative.

Interrogative Pronouns

The interrogative pronoun, as its name implies, introduces a question. **Quis** means *who,* and **quid** means *what.* Declension is like the relative, **quis** for **quī, quid** for **quod,** with the plural declined the same.

Possessive Pronouns (or Adjectives)

1st Person Sing.
meus, -a, -um my, *mine*
(Declined like bonus)

1st Person Plur.
noster, nostra, nostrum
(Declined like pulcher)

2nd Person Sing.
tuus, tua, tuum *your*

2nd Person Plur.
vester, vestra, vestrum

3rd Person Reflexive Possessive
suus, sua, suum *his, her, its, their*

Suus refers to the subject and agrees with the noun modified in gender, number, and case.

Reflexive Pronouns

The reflexive pronoun of the third person has a single declension for singular and plural, and all three genders.

Nom.	(none)	*Note:* The oblique cases of the
Gen.	suī	1st and 2nd person of the *per-*
Dat.	sibi	*sonal* pronouns are used ref-
Acc.	sē	lexively.
Abl.	sē	amō mē. *(I love myself.)*

The Intensive Pronoun Ipse

Ipse is used to emphasize nouns and pronouns of any person and agrees with the pronoun contained in the verb. Lēgātus **ipse** haec dīxit. *The envoy himself said these things.*

	Sing.			Plur.	
ipse	ipsa	ipsum	ipsī	ipsae	ipsa
ipsīus	ipsīus	ipsīus	ipsōrum	ipsārum	ipsōrum
ipsī	ipsī	ipsī	ipsīs	ipsīs	ipsīs
ipsum	ipsam	ipsum	ipsōs	ipsās	ipsa
ipsō	ipsā	ipsō	ipsīs	ipsīs	ipsīs

Relative Pronouns

Quī, quae, quod *(who, which)* is the most commonly used of the relative pronouns (or adjectives).

	Sing.			Plur.	
Masc.	Fem.	Neut.	Masc.	Fem.	Neut.
quī	quae	quod	quī	quae	quae
cūius	cūius	cūius	quōrum	quārum	quōrum
cui	cui	cui	quibus	quibus	quibus
quem	quam	quod	quōs	quās	quae
quō	quā	quō	quibus	quibus	quibus

Nominative Case

1. The subject of a finite verb is nominative. **Caesar** veniet. *Caesar will come.*
2. Predicate Nominative (Subject Complement). After the verb *to be* or any form thereof the subject complement replaces an object of the verb. It is in the same case as the subject. Herculēs **filius** Alcmēnae erat. *Hercules was the son of Alcmena.*

Vocative Case

1. The vocative case is used for direct address. Its forms are exactly like those of the nominative case, except for 2nd declension nouns ending in -us or -ius. Et tū, **Brūte!** *You, too, Brutus!* **Mī fīlī!** *My son!*

Genitive Case

1. Possession: Equus **Caesaris.** *Caesar's horse.* BUT: Equus **meus...** *My horse...* (Possessive adjective)
2. Quality (When a noun is modified): Vir **magnae virtūtis...** *A man of great courage.*
3. Subjective: Adventus **Caesaris...** *The arrival of Caesar.* (If the noun "arrival" were changed to a verb, *Caesar* would become the subject of it.)
4. Objective: Amor **pecūniae...** *The love of money...* (If the noun "love" were changed to a verb, *money* would be the object of it.) *Note:* These are nouns of action, agency, and feeling.
5. Partitive: Nihil **vīnī...** *No wine... (Nothing of wine),* Pars **exercitūs...** *Part of the army... Note:* The following adjectives modify their noun directly and are not followed by the genitive:
   omnis — *all of*   summus — *top of*
   tōtus — *whole of*   medius — *middle of*
   Cardinal numerals and quīdam take ex or dē plus the ablative case rather than the partitive genitive.
6. A possessive, partitive, or genitive of quality may stand in the predicate of a sentence. Hic gladius est **Caesaris.** *This sword is Caesar's.*
7. With verbs of remembering and forgetting. Ipse **mātris suae** meminerat. *He remembered (was mindful of) his mother. Note:* To remember or forget a *thing* is rendered by meminī plus the accusative case: **Omnia** meminit. *He remembers everything.*
8. Verbs of reminding take the accusative of the person and the genitive of the thing. Cicerō Catilīnam **facinōrum** admonēbat. *Cicero was warning Catiline of his crimes.*
9. Verbs of accusing or condemning take the genitive. Mē **inertiae** damnat. *He condemns me for laziness.*
10. With miseret, paenitet, piget, pudet, and taedet, the genitive is used as the cause of the feeling. Mē paenitet **inimīcitiae.** *I am sorry for my unfriendliness.*
11. Interest *(it is to the interest of)* and refert *(it interests)* take the genitive of the person. **Cicerōnis** intererat Clōdium morī. *It was to Cicero's interest for Clodius to die.*
12. With potior, sometimes the genitive is used instead of the usual ablative. **Oppidī** potītus est. *He took possession of the town.*
13. Preceding causā and gratiā *(for the sake of)* a gerund in the genitive or a noun modified by a gerundive, both genitive, is often used to express purpose. **Pugnāndī** causā, *in order to fight;* **urbis expugnāndae** causā, *in order to capture the city.*
14. Genitive of indefinite value is expressed by tantī *(of such value)*, quantī *(of how great value)*, magnī *(of great value)*, parvī *(of little value)*, and their comparative or superlative genitive forms. Est mihi **tantī.** *It is worthwhile (it is of such value) to me.*

Dative Case

1. Indirect object: **Fīliō** fābulam nārrāvit. *He told his son a story.*
2. Indirect object with an intransitive verb. Crēdite **mihi.** *Believe me.*
   Tibi persuādēbō ut discēdās. *I shall persuade you to go away. Note:* When these verbs are in the passive, the indirect object is retained, and the verbs become impersonal. **Tibi** persuādēbitur ut discēdās. *You will be persuaded to leave.*
3. Indirect Object with Compounds. Some verbs compounded with ad, ante, con, in, ob, post, prae, prō, sub, super in such a way as to change their meanings call for a dative object. Caesar Brūtum **exercituī** praefēcit. *Caesar put Brutus in charge of the army.*
4. Dative of Possession (with the verb *to be*). **Imperātōrī** est gladius. *The emperor has a sword.*
5. Dative of agent is used with the gerundive and some of the perfect passive constructions to show the "doer" of the action. Oppidum **Caesarī** est oppugnandum. *The town ought to be besieged by Caesar.* **Mihi** dēlīberātum est. *I have deliberated.*
6. Dative of Purpose. Vēnit **auxiliō** castrīs. *He came as an aid to the camp.* The following words are most commonly used with this construction:
   auxilium - *aid,* praesidium - *guard,*
   cūra - *care,* subsidium - *reserve*
7. Dative of Reference. The person or thing affected in the sentence **...quibus** locus parātur *...for whom a place is being made ready. Note:* When the datives of purpose and reference are used together, they are called the double dative. Flūmen erat **magnō impedīmentō Gallīs.** *The river was a great hindrance to the Gauls.*
8. Dative of Separation. Occasionally, after compounds with ab, dē, ex, ad, the dative occurs instead of the usual ablative. Hunc timōrem **mihi** ēripe. *Take this fear from me.*
9. The dative occurs with adjectives of *fitness* (aptus), *nearness* (proximus), *likeness* (similis), *friendliness* (amīcus), and their opposites. Gallī sunt proximī **Germānīs.** *The Gauls are near the Germans.*

Accusative Case

1. Direct Object of a transitive verb. Brūtus **Caesarem** vulnerāvit. *Brutus wounded Caesar.*
2. Subject of the infinitive. In indirect statements and after iubeō *(order)*, patior *(allow)*, and sinō *(permit)*, the subject of the infinitive goes into the accusative case. Dīxit **ducem** fūgisse. *He said that the leader had fled.*
3. Predicate accusative or object complement where a second accusative is used after appellō *(name)*, dēligō *(choose)*, creō *(make)*. Pompeium **cōnsulem** creāvērunt. *They elected Pompey consul.*
4. After verbs of asking and teaching, two accusatives are found: one of the direct object, the other the things asked or taught. **Mē sententiam** rogāvit. *He asked me my opinion.*
5. Time how long. **Multās hōrās** pugnāvērunt. *They fought for many hours.*
6. Extent of Space. **Multa mīlia** passuum iter fēcērunt. *They marched many miles.*
7. Object of certain prepositions. These prepositions take an accusative object: ad, ante, circum, contrā, inter, intrā, ob, per, post, prope, propter, super, trāns, ultrā. Per **hōs annōs...** *During these years...*
8. *Ad* with the accusative gerund or a noun modified by the gerundive, both accusative, is often used to express purpose. *Ad* **pugnandam,** *in order to fight; ad* **urbem expugnandam,** *in order to capture the city.*

Ablative Case

1. Object of certain Prepositions (all those not listed as governing the accusative case). The more common ones are: ā/ab, cum, dē, ē/ex, in, prae, prō, sine, sub.
2. Personal agent, expressed with a passive verb and a person, with ā/ab. Caesar ā **Brūtō** interfectus est. *Caesar was killed by Brutus.*
3. Separation. With a verb of motion, the ablative is always used. Hostēs ā **fīnibus** prohibent. *They keep the enemy from their territory.*
4. Place from which. Ex **urbe** ēgressus est. *He left the city.*
5. Ablative of Cause. **Timōre** commōtus est. *He was frightened (moved by fear).*
6. Ablative of Means. With the deponent verbs ūtor *(use)*, fruor *(enjoy)*, fungor *(accomplish)*, potior *(gain)*, and vēscor *(feed on)*, the ablative is usually used. **Gladiīs** ūsus est. *He used swords.*
7. With opus and usus (meaning *need*). Opus est **armīs.** *There is need of arms.*
8. Ablative of accordance. **Suā sponte...** *Of his own accord...* **Nostrīs mōribus...** *According to our customs...*
9. Ablative of place where (with *in* only). If *in* is omitted with names of towns, *domus, rūs,* and *humus,* the locative case is used (see below). In **urbe** est. *He is in the city.*
10. Ablative of Comparison. When quam *(than)* is omitted in comparisons, the ablative is used. Mare est altius **flūmine.** *The sea is deeper than the river.*
11. Specification. This ablative tells in what respect something is done or is true. Mōns magnus **altitūdine...** *A mountain great in height...*
12. Degree of Difference. After comparatives, this ablative shows the extent or degree to which the objects differ. Puer est altior quam puella **ūnō pede.** *The boy is taller than the girl by a foot.*
13. Ablative of manner, telling "how," may omit the usual cum if the noun is modified. **Magnā** (cum) **celeritāte** fūgērunt. *They fled with great speed.*
14. Accompaniment (regularly with cum). Cum **coniugibus...** *With wives...*
15. Ablative of means or instrument of an action occurs without a preposition in most cases. Mīlitēs **gladiīs** vulnerātī erant. *The soldiers had been wounded by swords.*
16. Ablative of time when, without a preposition. **Prīmō annō...** *In the first year...*
17. Ablative Absolute. This construction consists of a noun or pronoun in the ablative case plus a present active or perfect passive participle, or two nouns in the ablative case, or a noun and an adjective, with the participle understood. The construction is usually translated by a clause referring to time *(when)*, cause *(since, because)*, concession *(although)*, condition *(if)*. In any given instance any of the above translations may be appropriate, depending upon the sense of the rest of the context. **Mīlitibus** vulnerātīs, dux fūgit. *When the soldiers were wounded the leader fled.* (This could also be: *Because the soldiers...)*
18. Quality or Description. Vir **magnā virtūte...** *A man of great courage...*

Locative Case

The locative case is used only to indicate "place where" or "place at which" with names of towns or cities, humus *(soil)*, domus *(home)*, and rūs *(the country)*. In all other cases the ablative of "place where" with the preposition *in* is used. The locative endings are:

	Sing.	Plur.
1st Declension	-ae	-īs
2nd Declension	-ī	-īs
3rd Declension	-ī or -e	-ibus

Rōmae — *in Rome,* domī — *at home,*
rūrī — *in the country*

8. NUMERALS

Of the numerals, only ūnus, duo, trēs, the hundreds, and the plural of mīlle are declined.

	ŪNUS			DUO			TRĒS		MĪLLE
	M.	F.	N.	M.	F.	N.	M. & F.	N.	P. only
Nom.	ūnus	ūna	ūnum	duo	duae	duo	trēs	tria	mīlia
Gen.	ūnīus	ūnīus	ūnīus	duōrum	duārum	duōrum	trium	trium	mīlium
Dat.	ūnī	ūnī	ūnī	duōbus	duābus	duōbus	tribus	tribus	mīlibus
Acc.	ūnum	ūnam	ūnum	duōs	duās	duo	trēs (-īs)	tria	mīlia
Abl.	ūnō	ūnā	ūnō	duōbus	duābus	duōbus	tribus	tribus	mīlibus

There are four types of numerals: Cardinal Numerals (adjectives) one, two, etc.; Ordinal Numerals (adjectives) first, second, etc.; Distributives (adjectives) one by one, two by two, three each, etc.; Numerical Adverbs (once, twice, etc.).

	Cardinals	Ordinals	Distributives	Adverbs	Numerals
1	ūnus, -a, -um	prīmus, -a, -um	singulī, -ae, -a	semel	I
2	duo, duae, duo	secundus	bīnī	bis	II
3	trēs, tria	tertius	ternī (trinī)	ter	III
4	quattuor	quārtus	quaternī	quater	IV
5	quīnque	quīntus	quīnī	quīnquiēns	V
6	sex	sextus	sēnī	sexiēns	VI
7	septem	septimus	septēnī	septiēns	VII
8	octō	octāvus	octōnī	octiēns	VIII
9	novem	nōnus	novēnī	noviēns	IX
10	decem	decimus	dēnī	deciēns	X
11	ūndecim	ūndecimus	ūndēnī	ūndeciēns	XI
12	duodecim	duodecimus	duodēnī	duodeciēns	XII
13	tredecim	tertius decimus	ternī dēnī	terdeciēns	XIII
14	quattuordecim	quārtus decimus	quaternī dēnī	quater deciēns	XIV
15	quīndecim	quīntus decimus	quīnī dēnī	quīndeciēns	XV
16	sēdecim	sextus decimus	sēnī dēnī	sēdeciēns	XVI
17	septendecim	septimus decimus	septēnī dēnī	septiēns deciēns	XVII
18	duodēvīgintī (octōdecim)	duodēvīcēsimus (octāvus decimus)	duodēvīcēnī (octōnī dēnī)	duodēvīciēns (octiēns deciēns)	XVIII
19	ūndēvīgintī (novendecim)	ūndēvīcēsimus (nōnus decimus)	ūndēvīcēnī (novēnī dēnī)	ūndēvīciēns (noviēns deciēns)	XIX
20	vīgintī	vīcēsimus	vīcēnī	vīciēns	XX
21	vīgintī ūnus	ūnus et vīcēsimus	vīcēnī singulī	vīciēns semel	XXI
30	trīgintā	trīcēsimus	trīcēnī	trīciēns	XXX
40	quadrāgintā	quadrāgēsimus	quadrāgēnī	quadrāgiēns	XL
50	quīnquāgintā	quīnquāgēsimus	quīnquāgēnī	quīnquāgiēns	L
60	sexāgintā	sexāgēsimus	sexāgēnī	sexāgiēns	LX
70	septuāgintā	septuāgēsimus	septuāgēnī	septuāgiēns	LXX
80	octōgintā	octōgēsimus	octōgēnī	octōgiēns	LXXX
90	nōnāgintā	nōnāgēsimus	nōnāgēnī	nōnāgiēns	XC
100	centum	centēsimus	centēnī	centiēns	C
101	centum ūnus	centēsimus prīmus	centēnī singulī	centiēns semel	CI
200	ducentī, -ae, -a	ducentēsimus	ducēnī	ducentiēns	CC
300	trecentī	trecentēsimus	trecēnī	trecentiēns	CCC
400	quadringentī	quādringentēsimus	quadringēnī	quadringentiēns	CCCC
500	quīngentī	quīngentēsimus	quīngēnī	quīngentiēns	D
1000	mīlle	mīllēsimus	mīllenī	mīlliēns	M
2000	duo mīlia	bis mīllēsimus	bīna mīlia	bis mīlliēns	MM

9. PREPOSITIONS, PREFIXES

Most of the prepositions in Latin are used to govern the use of the accusative case. About one third of them govern the ablative, and a few govern both cases, depending upon the verb used in the sentence (see Syntax of Verbs, page 4). Many prepositions are also commonly used as prefixes. Attached to the front of a word, they give it a different shade of meaning. Examples are below.

Preposition	Case	Meaning	Derivative	Meaning
ā, ab	Ablative	*away from*	**ab**dūcō	*lead away*
ad	Accusative	*to*	**ad**dūcō	*lead to, influence*
ante	Accusative	*before*	**ante**cēdō	*go before*
apud	Accusative	*at, among*		
circum	Accusative	*around, about*	**circum**ferō	*carry around*
contrā	Accusative	*against*	**contrā**dīcō	*speak against*
cum, con, com	Ablative	*with*	**con**trahō	*draw together*
dē	Ablative	*down from*	**dē**scendō	*climb down*
ē, ex	Ablative	*out from*	**ex**pellō	*drive out*
in	Accusative	*into*	**in**iciō	*hurl into*
in	Ablative	*in (place where)*		
inter	Accusative	*between, among*	**inter**mittō	*interrupt*
ob	Accusative	*on account of*	**oc**currō	*run to meet*
per	Accusative	*through*	**per**rumpō	*break through*
post	Accusative	*after*	**post**pōnō	*put after*
prae	Ablative	*in front of*	**prae**ficiō	*put in command*
praeter	Accusative	*along by, past*	**praeter**eō	*go past*
prō	Ablative	*in front of*	**prō**fundō	*pour forth*
propter	Accusative	*on account of*	**propter**eā	*on that account*
re-, red-	Prefix only	*back*	**red**imō	*buy back*
sub	Accusative	*up from under*	**sub**vertō	*upset*
sub	Ablative	*under*	**sub**trahō	*draw from under*
super	Accusative	*above*	**super**gredior	*step over*
trāns	Accusative	*across*	**trāns**eō	*go across*
ultrā	Accusative	*beyond*	**ultrā**mundānus	*out of this world*

10. FORMATION AND COMPARISON OF ADVERBS

Positive adverbs are formed regularly by adding **-ē** to the base of adjectives of the 1st and 2nd declensions (longē). Adjectives of the 3rd declension may be changed to adverbs by adding **-iter** to the base (fortiter). Those with a base of **-nt** simply add **-er** (prūdenter). Examples are below.

Positive	Comparative	Superlative
longē	longius	longissimē
fortiter	fortius	fortissimē
miserē	miserius	miserrimē
ācriter	ācrius	ācerrimē
facile	facilius	facillimē
prūdenter	prūdentius	prūdentissimē
bene	melius	optimē
male	pēius	pessimē
magnopere	magis	maximē
multum	plūs	plūrimum
parum	minus	minimē
diū	diūtius	diūtissimē

Adverbs of Location

hīc (*here*)	hinc (*hence*)	hūc (*hither*)
ibi (*there*)	inde (*thence*)	eō (*thither*)
illīc (*there*)	illinc (*thence*)	illūc (*thither*)
istīc (*there*)	istinc (*thence*)	istūc (*thither*)
ubi (*where*)	unde (*whence*)	quō (*whither*)

hāc (*by this way*)	usquam (*anywhere*)
eā (*by that way*)	nusquam (*nowhere*)
illā (*by that way*)	intrō (*inwardly, from the outside in*)
istā (*by that way*)	
quā (*by what way*)	extrō (*outwardly, from the inside out*)
ultrō (*beyond*)	

Adverbs of Time

prīmum (*first*)	iam (*already*)
deinde (*next*)	iam diū (*long ago*)
semper (*always*)	iam nōn (*no longer*)
umquam (*ever*)	prīdiē (*the day before*)
numquam (*never*)	saepe (*often*)
cum (*when*)	hodiē (*today*)
ut (*when*)	cotīdiē (*daily*)
quandō (*when?*)	herī (*yesterday*)
mox (*soon*)	crās (*tomorrow*)
dum (*while*)	nōndum (*not yet*)

Interrogative Adverbs

-ne, an enclitic, expects the answer "*maybe.*"
Ēnumerābis**ne** puerōs? (*Will you count the boys?*)
Nōnne expects the answer "*yes.*"
Nōnne ībis? (*You will go, won't you?*)
Num expects the answer "*no.*"
Num manēbis? (*You won't stay, will you?*)
An, -ne, anne, utrum, num, introducing indirect questions, all mean "*whether.*"
Nesciō utrum veniam **an** eam. (*I don't know whether I'm coming or going.*)

Negative Adverbs (Particles)

nōn (*not*), nē, in a prohibition (*not*)
haud (*not*), nē, in a purpose clause (*lest*)
minimē (*not at all*), nē, after verb of fearing (*that*)
nec, neque (*and not*) nēve, neu (*and not*)
neque...neque, nec...nec (*neither...nor*)
nē...quidem, with the emphasized word between (*not even*)
nōn sōlum...sed etiam (*not only...but also*)
nē quis, nē quid (*so that no one, so that nothing*)

Relative Adverbs

Relative adverbs introduce certain clauses:
ubi (*where*) Nesciō **ubi** puer sit. (*I don't know where the boy is.*)
quō (*whither*) cognōvī **quō** fūgisset. (*I learned whither he had fled.*)
unde (*whence*)
cum (*when, since, although*)
quārē (*why*)

Adverbs of Degree

quam (*how*)	ergō, itaque, igitur (*therefore*)
tam (*so*)	proptereā (*on this account*)
paene (*almost*)	ita, sīc (*thus, so*)
ut, utī (*how*)	cūr, quārē (*why*)

Card Storagebox Bottom

Assembly Instructions

This is the inside of the box.

1. Cut out the pattern following the outside lines.

2. Cut along the solid lines between the A tabs and B sides.

3. Prefold the box along all of the dashed lines.

4. Glue the A tabs to the inside of the B sides. Alternately you may tape the tabs down, and apply additional tape to the outside corners to hold the box together.

BOX BOTTOM

Catullus Vocabulary Cards for AP* Selections
Bonus: Graphic Latin Grammar Cards
by David R. Pellegrino

185 vocabulary cards from the AP* Selections of Catullus. All vocabulary occurring five or more times is included on the cards. Cards are bound into book form and printed on perforated cardstock, with easily assembled storage box. Bonus removable full-page cards for quick reference while reading: Full AP* selections vocabulary list • *Graphic Latin Grammar* • Meters of Poems • Metrical Terms, Tropes or Figures of Thought, and Rhetorical Figures or Figures of Speech

ISBN 978-0-86516-653-0

Card Storagebox Top

A

fold

fold

A

cut

fold

cut

glue
A
here

glue
A
here

Assembly Instructions

This is the inside of the box.

1. Cut out the pattern following the outside lines.

2. Cut along the solid lines between the A tabs and B sides.

3. Prefold the box along all of the dashed lines.

4. Glue the A tabs to the inside of the B sides. Alternately you may tape the tabs down, and apply additional tape to the outside corners to hold the box together.

B

fold

fold

B

glue
A
here

BOX TOP

glue
A
here

cut

fold

cut

A

fold

fold

A

ISBN: 978-0-86516-653-0

CATULLUS
VOCABULARY CARDS
for AP Selections*

CATULLUS VOCABULARY CARDS *for AP* Selections*

CATULLUS VOCABULARY CARDS *for AP* Selections*

DAVID R. PELLEGRINO

Bolchazy-Carducci Publishers, Inc.
1000 Brown St., Unit 101, Wauconda, IL 60084
Phone: (847) 526-4344; *Fax:* (847) 526-2867
www.bolchazy.com